Contextual Theology:

Voices of West African Women

Contextual Theology:

Voices of West African Women

**Edited by
Meehyun Chung**

Tercentenary Publication
2010

Contextual Theology: Voices of West African Women- Published
by the Rev. Dr. Ashish Amos of the Indian Society for Promoting
Christian Knowledge (ISPCK), Post Box 1585, 1654, Madarsa Road,
Kashmere Gate.

© Author, 2010

*The views expressed in the book are those of the author and the publisher takes no
responsibility for any of the statements.*

ISBN: 978-81-8465-105-8

Cover Design: Yongho, Jeung (Student, Kaywon School of Art and
Design, Korea)

Cover Photo: Myungoh Chung (Professor, Kaywon School of Art and
Design, Korea)

ISPCK, Post Box 1585, 1654, Madarsa Road, Kashmere Gate,
Delhi-110006 • *Tel:* 23866323

e-mail: ashish@ispck.org.in • ella@ispck.org.in
website: www.ispck.org.in

Contents

Foreword

It is a universal and undeniable fact that women have the greater merit in passing the Christian faith on from one generation to the next. It was, and is, women who carry the greater load of voluntary work in the congregations - no matter on which continent they live. The other well-known and undeniable fact is that in spite of that, men have mostly been the ones in leadership. Great Christian names, well documented and recorded in the history books, are usually male names. The only exceptions are in times of spiritual awakening, pioneer situations, or moments of heavy distress and persecution when women were more free to express their full potential in the church.

There still are those who find the exclusion of women from pastoral ministry and leadership a matter of natural, God-given order or foreign to their culture. I disagree. I disagree not only for theological reasons but based on real experiences. I have worked with so many gifted, industrious and spirit-led women pastors that it is simply unthinkable for me not to count on women's capacities in ministry and leadership. People of both genders share the same high calling, and it is the same Divine Spirit of Christ who wants to work through both men and women for the benefit of people, and the Glory of God. "Can anyone keep these from being ordained? They have received the Holy Spirit just as we have." I would like to echo the apostle Peter's comment about the baptism of non-Jews (Acts 10:44-47).

I can boldly argue like I do, because different from many male leader colleagues in West Africa and elsewhere, I have had the privilege of being trained and ordained as a minister when most Protestant churches in my cultural environment were already ordaining women for the pastoral ministry. But there is no reason for boasting. Women's ordination is a very recent phenomenon also where I live. The first Protestant regional church in the German speaking world ordained women in 1927; the last regional one only in 1991 when I was already pastoring a congregation. Many of us Europeans tend not to remember how recent these developments really are.

Looking at the manuscript and listening to the "voices from West African Women," one can learn of the amazing depth and impressive breadth of experience and reflection of women in that part of the world. I congratulate my colleague Meehyun Chung, and all who have contributed to this collection of profound texts. May they not only communicate the respective subjects dealt with as such, but also convey the message behind the text: It is time to let women in all places reach their potential as theologians and pastors. God's Spirit, renewer of church and world, works through them as well as through us men, called into the same service and mission.

Rev. Martin Breitenfeldt
Director mission 21
15th Sep. 2010
Basel, Switzerland

Preface

This book is a collection of articles written by female theologians from Cameroon and Nigeria among the partner churches (the Presbyterian Church of Cameroon and Church of Brethren in Nigeria) of mission 21. Mission 21 has had a relationship with these two churches through the Basel mission since 1886 and 1959, respectively.

Compared to previous decades, there are a good number of female pastors and theologians. Although the Church of Brethren in Nigeria still does not allow women's ordination, they, also, have well prepared promising female theologians. My sincere hope is that they could serve in their church as ordained pastors in the very near future.

Every theology is related to its own local context and time. Especially, these articles reflect on their own context, where the writers are living and struggling. One of my main tasks in mission 21 is to promote women's voices in theology from a global southern perspective and to make their voices both audible and visible. This book covers the following subjects: Health and healing (Safiya Doma, Perpetua Fonki) Women's ministry (Roseline Luka Vandi, Suzan Mark Zira) Elimination of poverty and community development (Kanadi Dauda Gava, Rebecca. S. Dali, Eta Eyolle Elvira) Challenge of reconciliation in religious and ethnical conflicts (Koni Patrick, Azange Margaret) and Overcoming social and cultural problem regarding polygamy (Mary Nyampa).

My deep appreciation to all contributors for their efforts and my hope that this is a small token of empowerment through writing, reading and acting together.

Rev. Dr. Meehyun Chung

June 25, 2010, Basel

Educational Response to HIV Prevention Among Nigerian Girls

Safiya Doma

INTRODUCTION

Nigeria has recorded some progress in reducing the rate of HIV infection however cases of new infections, and inadequate supply of life sustaining retroviral therapy for people who are already infected show that the drop in prevalence does not really mean that the spread of HIV has been effectively curtailed. Sero-prevalence surveys indicate that fifty percent of the new infections are among young people aged 15-29, with heterosexual transmission as the predominant mode of infection. At the centre of the epidemic are girls and young women who are made more vulnerable to HIV infection by poverty, socio-cultural, religious, gender and political factors. These challenges will continue to pose great dangers for young girls unless there is an individual/societal change in sexual behaviour and girls are equipped with the skills and resources to protect themselves from HIV infection.

Everyone is at risk of HIV infection but this work focuses on girls because their biological make-up[1] along with other factors

---

[1] Carolyn Baylies "Cultural Hazards Facing Young People in the Era of HIV/AIDS: Specificity and Change" in eds. Nana K. Poku & Alan Whiteside, *The Political Economy of AIDS in Africa*, (England:

make them more susceptible to HIV infection than others. This work gives a brief overview of Nigeria's AIDS situation, reviews some of the response efforts on HIV prevention for young people and discusses why an educational approach is feasible in curtailing the AIDS epidemic. In view of the multi-dimensional nature of the HIV& AIDS epidemic and the contextual challenges girls face, the concluding part discusses HIV prevention framework that engages all the different layers of their vulnerability to HIV infection.

An Overview of the Nigerian Situation

With a population of about 150 million, Nigeria has the second largest burden of HIV&AIDS in sub-Saharan Africa. It is estimated that there are about 1.8 million AIDS orphans and 2.9-3.3 million people living with AIDS, 57% of which are females. There are geographical variations of HIV prevalence rates within the regions suggesting that while it appears to be under control nationally, the epidemic is still raging in some regions. The simple reason for this is a combination of some or all the factors discussed below

Poverty

Nigeria's poverty profile shows that despite the abundance of resources in the country, about 60% of the total population are poor while only 20% of the population own 65% of the nation's wealth. As income varies according to gender, region, education, age and occupation, there is higher poverty prevalence among females in the North Eastern region of the country than in other regions. Poverty is characterized by lack of basic needs required for healthy spiritual, emotional, and physical development of the individual. It is a situation where children lack access to enough resources to grow healthy and strong, to get education, to live in

---

Ashgate Publishing Ltd., 2004), 5. See also Anne Bayley, *One Humanity: The Challenge of AIDS.* SPCK International Study Guide (Cambridge: The University Press, 1996).

a good and safe environment and to fulfil their potential.[2] Poverty provides a fertile ground for the epidemic to thrive because it means more people are migrating to the cities in search of non existent greener pasture and when families are separated, the temptation to indulge in casual sex arises. When people are poor, even condoms become too expensive and they throw caution to the wind by engaging in activities that expose them to the risk of HIV infection.

Politics

Politically, Nigeria has leadership crises. Some of the leaders have been involved in corruption and plundering of the nation's resources along with other international collaborators. Nigeria's poverty which is avoidable is a direct consequence of corruption, money laundering and lack of political will by the government to ensure the equitable distribution of the national resources and to provide basic infrastructure like good roads, power supply, functional schools and standard healthcare systems. Failure of the government to provide quality education, employment, and recreational facilities for the majority of youths has created a situation where self serving politicians manipulate them to their advantage. It is this class of angry largely urban youths that politicians incite and recruit to enable them crush their perceived enemies and to ensure their control over resources. The fight for the available scarce resources results in the frequent religious and ethnic violence, a factor which continue to hamper any meaningful development or provision of sustainable programmes to control the spread of HIV&AIDS.

Culture & Gender

Though gender refers to both men and women, the experiences highlighted in this work mostly reflect the situation of girls and

---

[2] Human Development Report Nigeria 2008-2009, 69.

young women. According to the findings of a survey carried out by Danfulani Kore among 34 ethnic groups in Nigeria, women have a lower status than men.[3] Of course there are over two hundred and fifty ethnic groups in Nigeria and one cannot draw conclusions based on the findings on 34 cultures only, nevertheless, it provides a clue of the general power differential between males and females. We see the power imbalance between males and females in certain cultural practices like female genital mutilation and violence against women which are designed to control their sexuality. Nigerians are very hospitable by nature and in some cases women and girls end up being exposed to vulnerable situations where they are taken advantage of. Forced early marriages for girls and poligyny all put females in situations of powerlessness and vulnerability to HIV infection. Though women are the custodians and the ones who enforce these harmful practices, they are definitely not the direct beneficiaries. Gender constructions and stereotypes, double sexual standards for boys and girls and the association of masculinity with unnecessary display of prowess, violence, control, sexual risk-taking continue to harm both the men and women.

Religion

Religions are sometimes used to validate even actions that are retrogressive and harmful to everyone's well-being. It is not too difficult to find resources in Christianity or African Traditional Religions to justify cultural claims since there are interesting parallels at least, between some myths and biblical narratives. For example, in the biblical account, sin and suffering came into the world because Eve, a woman who succumbed to temptation and ate of the forbidden fruit African. One of such parallels is found in the myth about an old woman who used a mortar and

---

[3] Danfulani Kore, *Culture and the Christian Home*, (Jos: ACTS Publication) 1995, 4.

pestle to pound and each time she raised the pestle, it hit God and he moved farther and farther away from the earth until he went to the skies. When the woman and her colleagues realised what had happened, they attempted to bring God back to their midst by piling the entire mortars one on top of another to form a ladder to reach God. These were not enough because they needed just one more mortar. The woman then suggested that they remove the first mortar at the bottom to put it on top. This was done, and the whole construction collapsed on them and many people were killed.[4]

The usual traditional interpretation of this story leads to the stereotyping of women as foolish and culpable in bringing about suffering on humanity because they caused God to go farther away from humans. The explanation for the AIDS crises in some quarters is women are materialistic, they are indulging in transactional sex and are seducing men through their indecent dressing. Since they claim that women are the culprit in the spread of AIDS, they argue that the epidemic will come to an end when women stop being materialistic, do not engage in transactional sex and cover every part of their bodies like masquerades. Unfortunately, this line of reasoning depict men as victims and it encourages them not to take moral responsibility for their culpability in the spread of HIV. What never fails to amaze me in the two stories is why men who are supposedly strong and wise are always conspicuously absent at critical moments of decision making.

National Response Efforts

In the national response to the epidemic, the Federal Government of Nigeria set up the National Agency for the Control of AIDS

---

[4] Lloyda Fanusie "Sexuality and Women in African Culture" in: Mercy Oduyoye and Musimbi Kanyoro(eds.), *The Will to Arise. Women, Tradition and the Church in Africa,* (Maryknoll, NY: Orbis Books), 1996, 138-139.

(NACA) at the office of the president with budgetary allocations. It has also developed strategic frameworks and plans on key areas such as prevention, treatment, care and support and monitoring and evaluation together with input from major stakeholders. Along with the resources allocated by the government and in collaboration with international donors, funds for care, treatment and prevention programmes were made available. Under the multi-sectoral platform, NACA has expanded its network by empowering civil societies, faith-based organisations and the private sector to increase access to resources for HIV prevention, care and treatment services.

Responding to the government's call for an enabling environment to fight HIV across all sectors and concerned about the fact that students are among the high risk groups, the education sector has responded by educating young people about HIV&AIDS. A lot of effort and resources have been invested in strengthening capacity to respond to creating awareness about HIV&AIDS among young people. However frequent strike action of teachers have continued to hamper the sustainability, coordination and effective implementation and monitoring of the policies developed at the national level.

Some faith-based organisations have developed curricula specifically designed for young people. *Faith-based AIDS Awareness Programme for Senior Secondary Schools* is designed to be incorporated into religious curriculum of secondary school students. *Choices for Life: A Youth Peer Education Training Manual on Reproductive Health, HIV and AIDS*, is a training manual for peer educators, adolescent reproductive and sexual health, STDs and life skills for young people. Other faith-based HIV campaign literature designed for young people include *Sex Guide: What Youths Should Know about Sex and HIV/AIDS* and *Ten Great Reasons to Say No to Sex before Marriage.* The titles of the booklet are self explanatory. These two come in small sizes and are produced in both English and vernacular. *Yes to Life; No to AIDS* contains information about AIDS, how it is transmitted, how it can be avoided and it provides information about caring for people living with AIDS. These materials emphasise abstinence for youths, justifiably so because it is in line with the teachings of the Bible and remains the best weapon of HIV prevention.

However, we must not lose sight of the fact that some women are positive because they became infected by their husbands though they married as virgins and had never engaged in extra-marital relationship. Many HIV+ children became infected through mother-to-child transmission or transfusion of infected blood, others through sharing of sharp objects contaminated with infected blood during cult initiations ceremonies. What all these examples show is the fact that HIV infection is more than an individual's resolve to abstain. Girls and boys are capable of abstinence and they need to be encouraged to abstain but as long as the underlying factors fuelling the epidemic are not addressed, we may continue to witness new cases of infection.

HIV Prevention in Schools: A Guide is another important resource for young people which takes a pragmatic approach to HIV prevention. The book covers such areas like teaching about HIV prevention to learners, assessing students' vulnerability to HIV infection, preventing HIV infection from non-sexual modes, guidelines on preventing some initiators of sexual intercourse, use of condoms and life skills for HIV prevention, among others.

From the discourse above, it is clear that a lot of initiatives have already been expended in the fight to curtail the spread of HIV&AIDS. However, due to the complexity of the epidemic, HIV education cannot be a once and for- all intervention strategy hence the need for more concerted educational efforts.

HIV-Prevention Educational Response

Since the dominant route of HIV transmission in Nigeria is through heterosexual sex, why an education response to prevention? First, an educational response in reducing HIV infection is based on the premise that ignorance is a social disease. Though education is not a cure for ignorance, it acts as a vaccine that mitigates its harmful effects on girls. AIDS education can help reduce the about ignorance of HIV & AIDS, enable individuals to identify the factors of their vulnerability, dispel myths and help overcome stigma and discrimination against people living with AIDS. Ignorance is a great handicap and it robs its victims of the true and correct picture of a situation. For example, some of the factors causing people to stigmatize and discriminate against people living with AIDS is the fear that if a person shakes hands with them, he or she runs the risk of becoming infected. As a social vaccine, education has the potential of greatly reducing the harmful effects of ignorance through the provision of accurate scientific information on the mode of HIV transmission. It also provides information how to avoid infection and where to access information and services on reproductive rights, STI treatments and retroviral therapy to extend the life of those who are infected.

Second, since education is a key correlate of poverty, the higher the level of an individual's education, the better the bargaining power and the access to high wage-jobs. The more education an individual has, the more the chances of moving out of abject poverty and becoming fairly economically self sustaining. I admit that this may not be a very strong argument because there are many Nigerian graduates without jobs; nevertheless education is key to reducing poverty which fuels the transmission of the virus. Equal educational opportunities for both boys and girls has the long term effect of equipping them to move out of poverty and reducing the incidence of desperate situations that push them into exchanging sex for favours or money. The global trajectory of the epidemic highlights the fact that it is more concentrated in areas where there is abject poverty and less options for personal choices.

Third, education has the potential of shaping and moulding the character of an individual and the society to make wise and informed choices that may result in change of behaviour. Studies have shown that the spread of HIV is lower with increasing education,[5] probably because functional education provides an individual with skills and resources not only to protect oneself from HIV infection but also to face the broader challenges of life. Though girls are not passive victims of societal influence, effective education that brings about a change in their behaviour must be directed at both the individual and social levels. Education initiatives for HIV prevention programmes do not automatically lead to a sustained behaviour change nevertheless, as a preparatory step, it prepares the ground for the provision of skills, resources, social changes needed for risk reduction strategies.

Framework for Effective HIV Prevention

In view of the complexity of the AIDS epidemic, there have been different approaches to HIV prevention strategies. One of the most feasible approaches in understanding the framework for HIV prevention is the one developed by CAFOD a faith-based development agency. The writers thus argue for a HIV prevention framework which combines initiatives that mitigate the impact, reduce the risk and decrease the vulnerability factors of HIV infection.[6] The strengths of this approach is it simplifies HIV prevention framework using a problem tree and engages in prevention strategies from bottom to top and top to bottom. The trunk represents HIV epidemic, the impact of the epidemic on the

---

[5] 2005 National HIV/Syphilis Sero-prevalence Sentinel Survey among Pregnant Women, Federal Ministry of Health, National AIDS/STDs Control Programme, April 2006.

[6] Ann M Smith et al., HIV Prevention from the Perspective of a Faith-Based Development Agency, CAFOD, London, 2004, *www.cafod.org.uk/policy* and Analysis/Policy Papers/HIV/AIDS/HIV Prevention, 2.

individual and the society is illustrated in the leaves and branches and the roots depict the direct causes of HIV infection. The superficial causes is body fluids which act as vectors of infection and the deeper roots symbolise the personal and society-wide factors that increase an individual's vulnerability to infection.

Mitigating the Impact

To help curtail the spread of HIV, stigma and discrimination against people infected and affected by HIV&AIDS need to be addressed. Yet despite all the rhetoric and campaigns aimed at reducing stigma and discrimination against people living with HIV and those affected by it, the progress recorded remain relatively low. Stigma and discrimination against the 'other' is deeply ingrained in the mind of every individual and group and one of the manifestations is the feeling of superiority the individual or group feels over others not so privileged. It is this feeling of superiority over others that make affluent nations associate HIV with poorer nations, Churches associates HIV with promiscuity and adults associate it with juvenile unbridled sexual drive, all of which leave deep wound on the minds of people living with HIV&AIDS and hamper the effectiveness of prevention strategies. Though poverty, promiscuity and juvenile sexual explorations contribute to the prevalence of HIV infection in the country, these factors alone are superficial. Some of the questions that beg for answers are:

Why are so many Nigerians living in poverty in the midst of abundance? Why is morality abysmally low in the Church in Nigeria and why have elders failed to model appropriate sexual restraints for young people? The answers to these questions show that there is no single reason that will suffices because they are a combination of individual, societal and international factors. Stigma has made the fight against AIDS a difficult one and in order to mitigate the impact of the epidemic, there must be policy shift that address economic empowerment of people living with

HIV&AIDS and the structural economic inequalities in the world, specifically in Nigeria. There is need to provide care and support services and to involve them at all levels of decision making bodies that formulate policies on HIV prevention programmes. There is need to provide girls who are HIV+ a safe and hospitable space so that they can share their stories and contribute meaningfully on how to prevent the spread of HIV. In our frenzy to prevent the spread of HIV infection, we have sometimes paid very little attention to this wise African saying that "it is the owner of the roof that knows where the roof leaks" and gone ahead to design prevention strategies without collaboration with the target population for whom they are designed.

The association of AIDS with pictures of emaciated people who are on the verge of death that are projected on television screen or cover pages of newspapers provide wrong signals to the society. Such bleak and hopeless pictures reinforce stigma and discrimination which are contained in these Hausa HIV&AIDS euphemisms as *kwanan ka ya kare* meaning your days have come to an end or *kanjamau* meaning the slim disease. Such stereotypes are incorrect because being HIV positive is no longer the death sentence, at least for people who have access to retroviral drugs, care and support services. As people avoid having intimate physical encounters with sick looking people, they become careless and engage in unprotected intimate contacts with healthy looking people whom they perceive to be HIV negative but may actually be positive.

Reducing the Risk

Based on their contexts of vulnerability, girls have the capacity to choose on whether to abstain or use condoms in order to protect themselves against HIV infections. Instead of focussing only on individual risk reduction strategies, either through abstinence or the use of condoms, HIV prevention framework needs to be based on correct understanding of personal risks as well as the risks to others. It is hoped that this understanding will equip them with skills and resources to make choices on how to change their lives in order to reduce their risks and those of other people who are in contact with them to HIV infection. There is no one sure passport to HIV free life, therefore it is important to highlight some of the prevention strategies that are concerned with immediate protection depending on the individual's context of vulnerability:

All things being equal, abstinence is the best and most effective weapon of HIV prevention against sexual transmission, therefore there is need to encourage girls to abstain, avoid having unsafe sex with multiple partners and to delay their first sexual encounters. HIV prevention also involves a clear discussion on condoms which many experts claim that though not 100% safe, they greatly reduce one's chances of HIV infection when used consistently and correctly.[7] I am aware of the usual strong resistance and antagonism between group that advocate for abstinence only and pro condom advocates. All the arguments that each camp usually put forward are good however, there is need to move away from either of these solutions to a multi-faceted approach. Though experts argue that no conclusive studies have shown that the promotion and use of condoms influence promiscuous sexual behaviour,[8] we must be aware of the factors militating against the correct and consistent use of condoms. Such factors are poverty which results in lack of funds to purchase condoms or negotiate safer sex, the circumstances in which illicit sex is carried out and lack of information on consistent and correct use of condoms, all of which need to be taken into consideration.

To enhance the effectiveness of HIV prevention strategies, there is need for an overhauling or an improvement of the nation's healthcare system so that all private and public health institutions

---

[7] Armin Zimmermann, *The Compassion of the Lord is for Everybody: A Christian Course on HIV/AIDS*, (Basel: Mission 21), 2007, 24.

[8] *Ibid.*117.

practice universal safety precautions and procedures like safer blood transfusion, hygienic use of needles and screening for HIV prevention of mother to child transmission and other transmissible infections. When girls have STIs, they often feel shy to go for treatment and because STIs are asymptomatic in females they can remain undetected and untreated. Thus, more needs to be done not only to equitably reach all the Nigerian population, but also to ensure quality access to prompt treatment of STIs, voluntary testing and counselling services, for particular target group.

Decreasing the Vulnerability

Mitigating the impact and risk reduction alone are not enough to effectively curtail the epidemic because the problem analysis of the AIDS epidemic shows that other factors contribute in making the individual vulnerable to HIV infection. Though girls are not victims however, they are not totally immune from what is happening around them. Therefore, HIV prevention programme responses do not only lie with individuals alone but also with the home, church, government and the international community. Smith et al underscore some of the key areas that actors need to address in this vulnerability layer of HIV prevention framework as follows:

- Advocate for changes to legislation, culture, attitudes or practices that promote imbalances of power.

- Break the silence that colludes with situations of denial, stigmatisation, isolation or discrimination.

- Challenge specific instances of discrimination and injustice that occur in legislation, cultures, attitudes or practices.[9]

A cursory look at the issues highlighted buttresses the need

---

[9] Ann Smith *et al.*, 11.

for a multi-sectoral and multi-faceted approaches whereby individuals and institutions work together to dismantle the factors that hamper progress in reducing the vulnerability of certain most at risk groups. If Nigeria wishes to break down these barriers, there has to be changes from top to bottom and bottom to top among the actors. This section therefore highlights the three actors and some of the specific changes needed in the legislation to address stigma, discrimination, power imbalances and gender justice.

Government

Tackling corruption is one way that the government can greatly contribute in reducing socio-economic factors of people's vulnerability to HIV infection. The government needs to legislate laws that will improve the welfare of marginalised groups like rural farmers, invest in infrastructure in both urban and rural areas, provide employment for youths and reform the Nigerian police force to reduce extortion and extra judicial killings. This will help create peace, safety of lives and property and an enabling environment to fight AIDS.

Home

The home also has a lot to contribute in changing certain practices and attitudes, breaking stigma and challenging injustices that create power imbalances. This is because the home is the place where parents pass on to their children their social heritage based on their own educational experiences in religio-cultural patterns of child-rearing. Children, on their part learn as they observe and imitate their parents and the adults in their lives. The apparent disparities in the distribution of power we see in the society is learned from the home where girls are socialized to be obedient, gentle, shy, and soft spoken while boys are to be adventurous, strong and self-willed. These are excellent qualities and I do not wish to see girls being turned into boys or vice versa but when their socialisation reinforce gender stereotypes that create room for male dominance ideology, gender violence and exploitation by significant male or female figures, there is need for change. The need to re-examine our understanding of gender is important because at the heart of the HIV&AIDS epidemic is gender inequities. Given the importance of education in HIV prevention and enhancing one's career prospect in life, government needs to be prioritsed education of the girl child and transform the rot in the educational sector.

Since it is in the home that the child learns what it means to be male or female, let us briefly examine the Hausa[10] words for husband and wife because it emphasizes the point being made. While the wife is called *uwargida* meaning mother of the house, the husband is called *maigida* meaning the owner of the house. If the wife is the mother of the house, one would expect the husband to be the father of the house, but he is rather the "owner of the house". Whatever may be the reasons for the choice of these words to describe the position of the husband and the wife, the words 'mother' and 'owner' are certainly not synonyms! In many homes, girls are saddled with house chores while boys can go out to play football with his friends and this attitude is carried on to adulthood where men expect to be served. This situation leaves girls overworked, with less time to attend to their school work and engage in recreational activities.

To decrease girls' vulnerability to HIV infection, we need to break the superficial silence on issues pertaining to sex and sexuality in the home. It is incorrect to claim that there is total silence on these issues; however, what obtains is a situation where parents resort to ambiguity or the use of esoteric language when talking about sex to their wards. This is not an easy subject but considering the high price we are paying because of this gap in

---

[10] The Hausas live in the Northern part of the country.

knowledge, parents need to live up to their responsibility by providing their wards with scientifically and culturally appropriate sexuality education. Such education must include training in on how girls can cope with the physical challanges brought about by their sexual developments as well as other sublimatory outlets of sexual expressions.

Appropriate sexuality education should avoid painting it as evil, over romanticizing it or using scare tactics to prevent young people from exploration because none of these approaches are effective and correct. The fact is sexuality is created by God and it is beautiful, however, it needs to used in a responsible manner.[11] Sexuality education programmes should present factual information within a framework of values that relate to the goals, ambitions, emotions and relationships of the individual so that it will be meaning for girls. They need to be helped to clarify their values as well as develop moral reasoning so that as developed persons they can be able to apply biblical principles to issues confronting them not only in this area but in other areas of life.

Church

More commitment is needed on the part of the Church to prioritise the fight against HIV & AIDS, violence, corruption and poverty in the Nigerian society. The church can engage young people in reconstructing identities that place their sexual health at risk and increase their vulnerability to HIV&AIDS. What is most needed in this time of AIDS is a world where boys and girls live in mutual reciprocity with one another and not one where existing gender roles confer undue privileges on boys alone. There is need to equip them with life skills training that will enhance their better performance in the society. HIV prevention need not only focus on the AIDS epidemic only but it must be comprehensive

---

[11] Christine Gudorf, *Body, Sex, and Pleasure: Reconstructing Christian Sexual Ethics,* (Cleveland, Ohio: The Pilgrim Press), 1994, 53-54.

enough to deal with other areas so that girls and boys will be empowered to live life in abundance. In concluding I use the words of J. Garland who writes, "Knowing how vulnerable young girls are, it is cruel for us to leave them without the training, the knowledge and the determination needed to live in a way that avoids AIDS."[12]

BIBLIOGRAPHY

Bayley Anne. One Humanity: *The Challenge of AIDS.* SPCK International Study Guide, (Cambridge: The University Press), 1996.

Baylies, Carolyn, "Cultural Hazards Facing Young People in the Era of HIV/AIDS: Specificity and Change", in: Nana K. Poku and Alan Whiteside (eds.), *The Political Economy of AIDS in Africa*, (England: Ashgate Publishing Limited), 2004.

Campbell, Catherine, "*Letting them Die: Why HIV/AIDS Prevention Programme Fails,* (Oxford: University Press), 2003.

Danfulani Kore, *Culture and the Christian Home*, (Jos: ACTS Publication), 1995.

Downs, Perry G., *Teaching for Spiritual Growth: An Introduction to Christian Education,* (Grand Rapids, Michigan: Zondervan Publishing House), 1994.

Dube Musa, Adinkra! Four Hearts Joined Together: On Becoming Healing-Teachers of African Indigenous Religion/s in HIV&AIDS Prevention" in: Isabel A Phiri and Sarijini Nadar (eds.), *African Women, Religion and Health,*   (Maryknoll, NY: Orbis Books), 2006.

"Introduction " in: Musa Dube (ed.), *Other Ways of Reading: African Women and the Bible,* (Geneva: WCC Publications), 2001.

---

[12] Jean Garland, *AIDS is Real and it is in our Church,* (Bukuru, Jos: ACTS,2005),   ibid.

Family Life International. *Family Life Education: Teaching Youth about Reproductive Health and HIV/AIDS from a Christian Perspective*: Arlington, 2006.

Fanusie, Lloyda, "Sexuality and Women in Africa" in: Mercy Oduyoye and Musimbi Kanyoro (eds.), *The Will to Arise: Women, Tradition and the Church in Africa*, (Maryknoll: Orbis Books), 1996.

Garland, Jean. *AIDS is Real and its in our Church*. (Bukuru, Jos: ACTS), 2005.

Gudorf, Christine. *Body, Sex, and Pleasure: Reconstructing Christian Social Ethics*, (Cleveland, Ohio: The Pilgrim Press), 1994.

UNDP. *Human Development Report Nigeria: Achieving Growth with Equity*. 2008-2009. Kunhiyop, Samuel Waje, *African Christian Ethics*, (Kaduna: Baraka Press & Publishers Ltd.), 2004.

Maluleke, Tinyiko S., "Towards an HIV/AIDS-Sensitive Curriculum" in: Musa Dube (ed.), *HIV/AIDS and the Curriculum: Methods of Integrating HIV/AIDS in Theological Programmes*, (Geneva: WCC Publications), 2004.

Oduyoye, Mercy A. *Introducing African Women's Theology*, (Cleveland: Ohio: The Pilgrims Press), 2001.

Petrus, Anne John. *Sex Guide: What Youths Should Know About Sex and HIV/AIDS*, (Abuja: Zestdesigns), 2005.

Phiri, Isabel A. et al. (eds.), *African Women, HIV/ AIDS and Faith Communities*, (Pietermaritzburg: Cluster Publications), 2006.

Smith, Ann M. et al., HIV Prevention from the Perspective of a Faith-Based Development Agency, (London, England: Zimmermann, Armin. *The Compassion of the Lord is for Everybody: A Christian Course on HIV AIDS*, (Basel: Mission 21), 2007.

Polygamy as a Pastoral Challenge to the Nigerian Church and its Effects on Women and Children

Mary Nyampa

INTRODUCTION

In this paper I intend to discuss some of the problems of polygamy proposing that in view of its adverse effects on women it should be discouraged among Christians. Polygamy has affected women in Nigeria spiritually, socially, psychologically and economically in the home, church and society.

It is hoped that the paper will contribute toward the attempt to seek solution to the challenges of polygamy in EYN. The paper is significant because EYN does not yet have a uniform policy concerning the treatment of polygamists. While some local churches of EYN welcome polygamists fully into the Church community, other EYN churches treat them as the worse of sinners, often viewed as living in perpetual adultery. Some pastors even disallow polygamists from partaking in Holy Communion and refuse to name and dedicate children of second wives. In some Churches of EYN also, second wives are denied membership of Women Fellowship. These conflicting attitudes towards polygamists in EYN are sources of worry to the polygamists who remain uncertain as to their standing before God. As Gulla

Nghayiya says 'the polygamists get discouraged and wonder whether they will be saved on the last day.'[1]The lack of straightforward instruction in the Bible concerning polygamy further complicates the situation.

The Practice of Polygamy in the Ancient and Biblical Times

Polygamy is commonly understood as having more than one wife at a time. The practice of having more than a wife has been right from ancient times, before the Bible was written. And most of the reasons that enhanced polygamy in the ancient world, biblical time and today are similar. In the ancient world, polygamy was practised because marriage was seen as a norm and anyone who did not marry was seen as an outcast. It did not matter whether a woman was the first or second or third wife. What was important for her was to simply have a husband in order to earn respect in society. But it was not just marriage but a productive marriage that was encouraged.

John H. Walton and other authors explain that women in the ancient world obtained honor through marriage and children bearing.[2] Their inability to bear children was often seen as a sign of punishment. Thus, 'the woman's life in the family will be very tenuous if she had not borne children' and 'a barren woman could be and often discarded or ostracized or given a low status'.[3] Men in ancient times desired to have many children and therefore they married many wives. If one's wife could not give birth or gave birth to uniform sexes or she could not produce the number of children her husband expected of her, the man could take more wives. Thus as Walton has stated further, polygamy was practised as a result of 'an imbalance in number of female and male, the

---

[1] Interview, TCNN 20/10/09.

[2] Cf. The Bible Background Commentary, John H. Walton(eds.), (Downers Grove: IVP), 2000, 34.

[3] *Ibid.*

need to produce large number of children to work herds and/or fields, the desire to increase the prestige and wealth of a household through multiple marriage contracts and the high rate of death of females in child birth'.[4] Furthermore, in the case of nomadic and farming community, men married more wives so that they could attach a woman to each household because in those days one man could have multiple households. Among the monarchs, it was a means of making alliances with powerful families or nations.[5]

The biblical polygamy was started by Lamech as recorded in Genesis 4:19-22. He married Adah and Zillah, although why he involved in polygamy was not stated. Abraham was the second person who was forced into polygamy due to childlessness as recorded in Genesis 16:1ff. His wife Sarah wanted them to have their own child, who would be their heir, as it was the practice then. She encouraged her husband to sleep with her mistress called Haggai. When Haggai took in, she began to look down on Sarah which caused the peace and respect that once existed between them to cease. Thus, polygamy brought rivalry between the two women. The third case has to do with Jacob as narrated in Genesis 29:8-30. Initially, Jacob intended to have Rachel as his wife but after working for Laban for seven years as agreed, Laban refused to give Rachel in marriage due to a cultural reason, that no one is allowed to give the younger one while the older daughter is still unmarried. That led to Jacob's second wife. Jacob ended up with four wives instead of one as was his intention. Because Rachel who was barren gave her mistress to produce children for Jacob. While Leah out of jealousy again needed additional children through her mistress.

Both David and Solomon, kings of Israel were polygamists. God Himself told David he should have asked him for more wives

---

[4] *Ibid.*

[5] *Ibid.*

and he could have given him rather than taking Uriah's wife. Solomon married hundreds of wives from diverse cultural backgrounds. These records of polygamy in the Old Testament do not show approval or disapproval of the practice. Thus, the Bible reflects the common practice of the ancient Near East that having many wives was a norm.

The Causes and Practice of Polygamy in Nigeria

Traditionally as other African countries, Nigerians practise polygamy because it is permitted and promoted by most Nigerian ethnic cultures. This is not unique to Nigeria, 'polygamy existed all over Africa as an aspect of culture or/and religion'.[6] As a traditional man you are allowed to marry the number of wives you want irrespective of how you will cater for their needs. Polygamy is practised in Nigeria for reasons similar to those in the ancient Near East. I. Gaskiyane says that;

> there is a profound sense of obligation in every marriage to ensure the continuation of the extended family and clan. There is a desire to ensure support and care for the parent in their old age. This requires having many children especially the male child. Desire to have many workers on the farm. Desire to have male child if the man did not have from the first wife. Desire to overcome the loss of children through death. Desire to provide children to childless wives. Above all, culture demands that every adult should marry. Therefore a woman would prefer to be one of multiple wives than to be without husband and be considered a social out cast.[7]

In ancient African society 'tribal war contributed to the practice of polygamy because it was men that were killed in the war leading to many widows, so polygamy was the only solution'.[8] Mercy

---

6 'Polygamy'.*http//en.wikipedia.org/wiki/* 25/10/2009.

7 I. Gaskiyane, Polygamy: A Cultural and Biblical Perspective, (Carlisle: Piquant), 2000, 15-16.

8 I. Gaskiyane, 17.

Llerbare concurs says 'Tribe and clans in Nigeria commonly fought each other and of course, men were the primary victims. The ratio of men to women was unequal; so men were expected to have and support more than wife'.[9] Polygamy was seen as a thing of pride, recognition, wealth, status and respect. In such a culture, 'a man can only be considered a person of influence or leader if he has many wives and children'.[10] Any man that has one wife is seen as a lazy man.

Many women in Nigeria became second wives not out of wish but by force. A woman could be forced to marry a man because her family saw the man has wealth, he is neat, kind and caring. Among many ethnic groups in Nigeria, a woman could be forced to marry any of her deceased husband's relations as she is considered part of her husband's property. In some parts of Nigeria, a girl could be taken by force while fetching water or rearing animal or playing with her mates to become a second wife. However, there are women who enter into polygamous marriage willingly.

In Islam the practice of polygamy 'is a permission given in the Qur'an with worded moral restriction'.[11] That if you cannot love, care equally for them do not even attempt. Therefore

> polygamy is allowed for men with the specific limitation that they can only have up to four wives at any time, by considering the first wife's wishes. The Qur'an also states that men who choose this must deal with their wives as fairly as possible, doing everything that they can to spend equal amount of time and money on each one of them. [12]

---

[9] Ilerbare, Mercy, 'Practice of Polygamy in Nigeria', *www.helim.com/items/25/10/09.*

[10] I. Gaskiyane, 18.

[11] *Ibid.*, 25.

[12] 'Polygamy'.*http//en.wikipedia.org/wiki/ 25/10/2009*

By implication, if the husband can treat, care and love the four wives without discrimination, he could have multiple wives. While my focus is neither the practice of polygamy in African traditional religion nor Islam, it is important to mention them as they probably influence some Christians in Nigeria to become polygamists.

Most forms of Christianity in Nigeria do not approve of polygamy. However, there are some Christians who go into polygamy willingly because of 'cultural norms that exceed religious restrictions in their opinion'.[13] But generally some Christians go into polygamy in Nigeria due to reasons mentioned under traditional culture like lack of male child, childlessness, prestige, wealth, cultural demands, mistake in the first choice of a partner and sheer lust as mentioned by some of my interviewees and respondents. Ambrose Osita Nwigwe also states that some Christians involved in polygamy due to the following reasons: That 'many of these groups of people marry another wife for the sole reason that the first wife is medically proven barren and she agrees that her husband marry another wife'.[14] He adds 'that it is a considerable reason because any marriage without a child is considered a failure and a miserable relationship. A number of men marry second wives out of selfish motives. Such as unreasonable action wreck not only the first but the second marriage as well'.[15]

Polygamy in EYN

Polygamy was not a problem in EYN for some years back due to the background of the converts. Some of the early converts were

---

[13] Chippla. 'polygamy.' *Http://www.strudeltimes.it/polygamy.htm 25/10/2009.*

[14] Ambrose Otita Nwigwe, 'Causes and Effect of Polygamy: The Way Forward for the Church: A Case Study of Church of Nigeria (Anglican Communion) Abuja Diocese,' (TCNN: BD Project, 2009), 45.

[15] *Ibid.*

already polygamists before they got converted. These were allowed to remain polygamous enjoying full membership of the Church. Some of them were had a say in the Church especially in the eighties. However, the influence of culture continues to cause many members of the Church to go into polygamy.

Culture has caused even Christian women to become second wives. Dorcas James regrets that her mother became a third wife as a result of culture. She said after the demise of her father, her mother had no option but to become the third wife of another man. She was told to marry him because he had wealth, and influence in the society.[16] He was said to be caring and loving. Rifkatu Bitrus said her mother became the last wife of her father because the man was a wealthy man and neat.[17] My mother was kidnapped to become the second wife of my father which is permitted by the Kamwe culture. There are so many wives in my home town and who are members of EYN who found themselves as second wives as a result of childlessness.

Childlessness has led to several cases of divorce and remarriage even in EYN. For example, Grace Gulla was a first wife of her husband and a dedicated chorister but because she was childless, coupled with the pressure from the husband and the relatives of the husband, she left and became a second wife. Also, some young men have gone into polygamy in EYN Sometimes also just to fulfil their sexual desires. Sex then becomes the prime reason rather than true love as confirmed by Danfulani Kore that 'wives must satisfy their husband's desire but husband have no concern about satisfying their wives sexually'.[18] By implication if a wife cannot satisfy her husband sexually, she can be sent away and the man could marry another wife.

---

[16] Dorcas James, 'Interview' TCNN Bukuru 20/10/09.

[17] Rifkatu Sinika, 'Interview' TCNN Bukuru 20/10/09.

[18] Danfulani Kore, Culture and the Christian Home. (Lagos: Integrated Press Ltd.), 1995, 26.

Wrong choice in early marriage also contributes to the rate of polygamy in EYN. Wrong choice has to do with some parents who chose marital partners for their children without the consent of the children. That is some parents chose whom their sons or daughters are to marry. In the case of early marriage, some parents encourage their children to marry at earlier stage of their life. In the case of female children it is thought early marriage is preferred to going further in education 'so that they will not be exposed and be impregnated by some one'.[19] When young men and women who married as a result of pressure from parent grow older, they tend to think they are not compatible spouses and many have gone into fresh marriages as a result. For example my father was forced to take his first wife by his parent because the first wife was kind to his father; sweeping his environment, washing and cooking for them when he lost his wife. But at the end she really suffered because he did not love her in the first place. Some female folks thought that they have overgrown their marital age and therefore they married sugar daddies.

Looking from the above-mentioned causes and nature of polygamy in EYN, we can now conclude that there are different cases of polygamy in the EYN Church. How should EYN handle such cases? Meanwhile I wish to talk about the plight of polygamy on women and children before stating how to handle them.

The Effects of Polygamy on Women

The consequences of polygamy on women and children are numerous, but the researcher wish to classify them under the following headings: spiritual, psychological and economic effects.

---

[19] General view of women on causes of early marriage during the women fellowship general council held in Mubi, May 2009.

Spiritual Effects

The second wives are deprived of their spiritual right as followers of Christ. In some churches, they have been deprived of 'participating in holy communion and from dedicating their children' because the church felt they are rebellious and have violated the law of God. Ishaya Filibus Gwamma said that they are seen as sinners who will face the wrath of God at the last judgment.[20] While Bitrus Sinika noted they see themselves as sinners and as a result they have lost self-esteem.[21] Some are deprived of any right to be part of women groups in the Church. Those of them who join women fellowship are deprived of having uniforms, registering as full members, praying and contributing designated amount of money by the women fellowship. They do not experience real fellowship as such when they attend the Women fellowship.

At a meeting of women fellowship leaders held in July 2009, we were instructed not to collect money from the second wives in our fellowships and that we should not allow them to participate in any activity. Some of the polygamous women are very talented in singing and beating drums but nobody will allow them use any of such gifts. Thus, their God given talents are idle or some have died off. As a result they no longer have spiritual motivation to actively contribute in the worship life of the Church. Some no longer have interest in the things of God. Ibrahim Tari Ali maintains that 'some polygamous' women no longer participate in any group, spiritual ceremonies, or acting in the church. In fact, they always do not have interest.'[22]

---

[20] Ishaya Filibus Gwama, 'Interview', TCNN Bukuru 22/10/09.

[21] Bitrus Sinika, 'Interview', TCNN Bukuru, 22/1009.

[22] Ibrahim Tari Ali, 'Interview' TCNN Bukuru 24/10/09.

Nwigwe notes also that the rivalry which exists between first and subsequent wives are often transferred to women fellowship.

> 'The competition, rivalry, quarrelling, act of bad faith, cold war, fighting rival groups formation, which is evident in polygamy have been transferred to many churches (women fellowship). Sizeable members of the congregation of the church' (women fellowship) are from the polygamous homes. They try to transfer the scenario in the polygamous home to the church'.[23]

It could be that the first wives are the ones making rules that restrict second wives from full participation in the activities of the women fellowship as a way of revenge.

The spiritual depravity which second wives suffer affect their children as well. The child born to a second wife is deprived of dedication and naming in the Church, suffering as a result of the action of his parent. Did the child choose his parent? The response given by pastors is that during dedication who will stand with the baby, the father or the second wife? Because for them both are sinners. Ishaya laments that 'the church losses a lot of talents that would have been helpful in its development both spiritually and otherwise'.[24] Ibrahim adds that 'the church may loose a polygamous member to the devil as a result of discrimination against them.'[25] The church referred to as 'Amariya Yesus' (the bride of Christ) accepts polygamists. This is one is even better than reverting to traditional religion or Islam even though several others did so.

---

[23] Nwigwe, 80.

[24] Gwamma, 'Interview', TCNN Bukuru, 22/10/09.

[25] Ibrahim, 'Interview', TCNN Bukuru, 24/10/09.

Social Effects

Socially polygamy creates competition, rivalry, envy and jealousy among the wives and children. Mercy Llerbare says that 'there have been cases where strife and jealousy broke out amongst the wives and children making the home dysfunctional and pretty much difficult to live in'.[26] Protus O. Kemdirim agrees with what Mercy said when she states that 'polygamy is one of the traditional practices that is demeaning to a woman's status. It brings suffering and rivalries between co-wives as well as their children. Some women have to suffer in silence 'ending up growing old prematurely losing their interest in life and, sometimes, even losing their minds.'[27] My parents are typical example of what Mercy and Protus have said, I observed that strife and jealousy were common in the family. Each wife would try to please the man either through giving him money, nice food, or children at the expense of her life. The children of the first wife feel that they are the first children of the family; therefore everything in the house is theirs. Dorcas whose mother became a third wife after her father died, lamented that the children of the first two wives teased them that her mother killed her father and now they have come to their house to share their husband and the things in the family. She said their lives in the house were like hell on earth.[28] Ambrose adds that children of rival women have been indoctrinated by their mothers to hate right or oppose children of rival women in the home...'[29] In some polygamous families, 'wife and children can go without food because some husband fail to give food to their wives to be cooked.'[30] At the demise of

---

[26] Nwigwe, 80.

[27] Emmanuel Martey, 'Women and Culture in Contemporary Africa' in Women, Culture and Theological Education. Edited by Protus O. Kemdirim and Mercy A. Oduyoye, (Enugu: SNAAP Press), 1998, 43.

[28] Dorcas

[29] Ambrose, 50.

[30] Danfulani, 80.

the husband too, the wife who produced only female children will not get any share in what they have laboured for as co-wives nor her children. However, some culture do give little to the female children as Danfulani explained that 'male children generally have a very high economic inheritance. On the other hand the family inheritance that is passed on to female children is moderate.[31] Mercy also adds that there have been cases where sharing of the husband's estate after his death led to intrigues and murder plots' among the rival women.[32]

Above all, HIV/AIDS is most devastating effect of polygamous family. Because of the sharing of one husband by co-wives, the disease is spread easily. When a man has several wives and he cannot satisfy their sexual desires, some of them may begin to look for sex partners outside their marriage which puts them at the risk of getting effected with HIV. Sometimes it can get rid of the entire family leaving many children orphans or the parent can be alive but unproductive in the family. This will definitely affect the finances of the family leaving the children sometimes uneducated or improperly fed. Chipple says that

> HIV/AIDS is a problem in Nigeria and the practice of polygamy is one of those cultural idiosyncrasies that assist in spreading it. Thus, I do believe that culture should give way to common sense. And common sense should result in legislation that limits one man to one wife and one woman to one husband at a time.[33]

As Chipple has noted if our country can include in her constitution that one man, one wife it will go a long way in solving the problem of polygamy rather than the church itself. Like in the Western world 'polygamous marriage is not recognized and bigamy is considered a crime. Several countries also prohibit polygamy.'[34]

---

[31] *Ibid*, 79.
[32] Mercy.
[33] Chippla, 2.
[34] *http://en.wikipedia.org/wiki.*

There have been cases where children from the polygamous family became thieves in the society because they did not have proper care. Danfulani says that 'irresponsibility of some families has led to the unhappiness and even death of children.'[35] He lamented that:

> lack of parental love can result in low self-esteem and personal and personality disorders. Children become passive and indifferent in life, filled with fear, hatred, insecurity, tension, guild, depression, anxiety, an excessive need for love, powerful feelings of revenge and guilt. These children grow up to become unwanted elements of society.[36]

That is the condition of children who grow without proper care. When one man has too many children as a result of polygamy, it is not possible for him to carter for their needs especially in such a poverty stricken country as Nigeria.

Psychological Effects

Some women and children are depressed to the extent where some have killed themselves because of family pressure. For example, my stepmother killed herself because she discovered that she was pregnant for my father against her wish because he did not care for her and her children. It is her innocent children who suffer the consequences of her action and the memory of her tragic death may continue to disturb them, as they grow older.

Economic Effects

The second wife and her children are always at the receiving end in a situation where the children of the first or the first two wives have grown while her children are still small. While the first or the first two wives are increasing financially she will be

---

[35] Danfulani, 69.

[36] *Ibid.,* 70.

diminishing. For example in a given polygamous family that has a common farm, it is the children of the first wife that normally enjoy the produce because it is from that farm produce that they are fed and their school fees paid. At the point when this last wife needed the family help for feeding and paying of school fees for her own children-the situation may have changed. As it is often the case, the farmland may later be shared and each woman is expected to carter for her self and her children. This becomes difficult especially for the latest wife since her own children would still be in school by the time the women are asked to be on their own.

There are some cases where some women resort to witchcraft in order to gain favour from the man and this sometime result to either killing of the man or the first or the second wife visa-visa which worsen their economic situation.

Since polygamy creates such adverse effects especially on women and children, why do women still go into polygamous marriage? Is it because there are no enough men to marry them as some people have argued? Also what is pushing people into polygamy knowing fully its negative effects, and the stand of the Church? Sometimes even leaders of Women Fellowship who lost their husbands become second wives or concubines.

The Way Forward

Some have appealed to texts such as 'let us make man in our image, in our likeness…God created man in His image. He created them male and female…Gen.1: 26-27 to discourage polygamy. It is argued that the Bible teaches that marriage union is between one male and one female. God alone created marriage and intended it to be monogamous. Danfulani says the verb 'created' (bara) in Hebrew language means solely divine act'.[37] Therefore, God instituted marriage to be one-man one woman nothing more or

---

[37] *Ibid.,* 9.

less. God did not create marriage for our own sake alone but for his glory (Eph 3:14-15).

Norman Gestler has the same view when he says 'monogamy was taught by precedent in Old Testament. God gave Adam one wife; this set the precedent for the whole race to follow'.[38] God also told Moses that 'neither shall you multiply wives (Deut. 17:17). While these are valid observations, they have not convinced many people that polygamy is wrong especially in view of the examples of key Old Testament figures cited earlier who were polygamous.

We should also bear in mind that it is easy for one to profess Christ but it will take time and series of teaching before one will turn away from his former lifestyle or culture which as we have seen, has encouraged polygamy in Nigeria. As long as women are considered in our culture as inferior, objects of sex, worker or cheap labourers, child bearers polygamy would hardly stop even among Christians in Nigeria. I think the way forward is not simply to say the Bible teaches monogamy, but to teach that all human beings; men, women and children are divinely and equally created in the image and likeness of God. They have their source from God. Men and women and children, all possess soul, spirit and body and are fearfully and wonderfully designed by God as recorded in these passages (Gen. 1:26, 2:7, Ps.138:13).

As testified by these Bible references Gen.3:15, Eccl.7:20, Rom. 3:23-26, John 3:16, 1Jh 2:2, Heb 10:10, 12, 14, 18, Rom 5:15-21. Christ treats women with dignity granting them equability with men before God through the Gospel. Rather God made them to be one in Christ Jesus Gal.3:28, 1Pt.3:7. Emphasising this truth to

---

[38] Norman L. Geisler, Christian Ethics: Options and Issues, (Grand Rapids: Baker Academic), 1995, 281.

members of EYN will help restore the dignity of women and may stop men from taking too many wives for sex or labour or children bearing under the dictates of African traditional culture.

The issue of children in the traditional set-up and even now is still a problem among Christians. We need to teach people that children are blessings from God which He may decide to give to a couple as He wishes. From biblical perspective, God expects children to be catered for by their parents. In a situation where there are too many children, it is hard for parent to obey this instruction. African men who marry many wives for children should remember that God will hold them responsible if they do not provide basic necessities of life to these children as expected of them.

We also ought to teach members of EYN about Biblical perspective on prestige, wealth and recognition since these are other reasons for polygamy. The Bible clearly states that wealth is from God (1Chron. 29:12). Therefore if God predestined a person to be rich he does not need to have many wives and children to become rich. A woman does not need to become a second or third wife just because the man has money. The issue of prestige and recognition is not in the number of wives and children or property on possess. Meaningful living is possible in monogamous marriage. In fact you do not need to be married to be happy in life let alone a polygamous marriage.

CONCLUSION

I have discussed the meaning of polygamy, why people engage in the practice and its effects on women and children in EYN. My point is that it is not enough for the Church to say that one man, one woman only. The Church needs to address these effects as well as a means of talking the challenge of polygamy.

The Role of Women in Community Development: An Example from Gavva Area

Kanadi Dauda Gava

1. INTRODUCTION

Women have been involved in community development for a long period of time. Most times they are not mentioned but they are key figures of community action, women's role in community development has become increasingly important. In some communities, they have established themselves as leaders in community development and acquired the skills that have brought positive change to their communities. Women have contributed a lot in making better relationships in their roles in their communities. Even with the contributions they are making in their communities they face cultural, economics, and social barriers in leading the community. If we have a glance over the history, we will come to know that behind every successful man is a woman. Women have been regarded as fragile part of the society but they can play a very important role for the betterment of the society.[1] While their comprehensive approach has influenced the evolution and nature of community development, women's contributions have been neither widely acknowledge nor explicitly credited.[2]

---

[1] *http://www.yespakistan.com/HDF/Mardan/women-comm.asp*

[2] *http://www.eurojournals.com/ejsr.htm*

Writing about community development has been my desire for long. As Christians it is our wish to see that our communities are developed having the necessary things required for sustenance. As a woman from my experience of the community where am married to. I have seen how the community has been neglected by the government. It is my wish to write and contribute my own opinion toward community development. In this paper I will give a brief background of the community, look at the contribution of government, missionaries and theological and spiritual perspectives looking at the scriptures on community development.

If we come from outside the community, we must be aware that we are strangers and may not know or understand many of the elements and situations which take place there. We may come from very different situations. I come from a different community with that of my husband, but am not stranger to his own community since we are married for about ten years now. I have the experience of his community which is also my community by virtue of marriage.

2. DEFINITION OF COMMUNITY

The word 'community' is defined and applied in many ways. It can refer to geographic communities where members are based on region;[3] unit of social organizations such as worker and community associations;[4] cultural groups that can be identified through religions or races;[5] or virtual communities, where members main form of contact is through electronic media.[6] Communities of circumstance constitute another possible form of community.

---

[3] Ife, 1997; Maimunah Ismail, 2001.

[4] Ife, 1997; Maimunah Ismail, 2001.

[5] Maimunah Ismail, 2001.

[6] Ife, 1997.

Community Development

Another definition that is well accepted was developed by the United States International Cooperation (1956).[7] It emphasized the process where individuals in the community joined forces to plan and take actions regarding community problems. They identify community problems and needs, plan and conduct activities together using available community resources. They also sought outside help from government and private organizations. On the other hand, the United Nations (1975) indicated that community development is a process whereby the efforts of individuals in the community were combined with efforts of government and non-government bodies to improve and developed community socially, economically and culturally.[8]

The definition of community development presented in this discussion views locality as a place where people live and meet their common daily needs together. Community action serves as a catalyst for transforming this interaction into purposive efforts that contribute to the emergence of community.[9] Interaction among local people facilitates many conditions. It leads to the development of community by increasing awareness and allowing for community action. It is often the case that people are unaware of the problems and issues facing other community residents.

This interaction-based perspective focuses on the ways that local people come to understand common needs, and contribute to collective actions designed to meet these needs. People sharing a common territory tend to interact with one another over place

---

[7] as cited by Maimunah Ismail (1999).

[8] European Journal of Scientific Research , Euro Journals Publishing, Vol.23 No.3 (2008), pp.361-372, *http://www.eurojournals.com/ejsr.htm.*

[9] Wilkinson 1991; Luloff and Swanson 1995.

relevant matters.[10] Consequently, interaction at the local level provides the basis for the emergence of community and for designing programs to continue its development.

From an interactional perspective, community development is seen as a dynamic process involving diverse social groups. In all localities, numerous distinct groupings of people are present.

This interaction allows for the emergence of community, which is an encompassing field that pursues the general interests and needs of the locality.[11] Through this process, local people are linked more inclusively together and motivated to focus on a wider range of community needs and wants. The relationships that are established and maintained increase the adaptive capacity of people who share a common territory. This adaptive capacity is reflected in the ability of people to manage, utilize, and enhance those resources available to them in addressing local issues.[12]

'It is strange that when people think about 'a community' they often think mostly about women and children and when people think about 'development' they often think mostly of men....In both urban and rural communities in the developed and developing world, not only is it the women who usually care for both the young and the old, but also they procure key resources such as water and fuel and are involved in agriculture and livestock production, and trading activities.....all which are necessary for the survival of the family unit'.[13] It is becoming increasingly realised that community development cannot separate itself from women. The UN decade for women (1976-1985) highlighted the importance of women in the development process, establishing that women perform two thirds of the

---

[10] Wilkinson 1991.

[11] Wilkinson 1991; Luloff and Bridger 2003.

[12] Wilkinson 1991; Luloff and Bridger 2003.

[13] Lovel et al, 1985.

world's work, receive only ten percent of the world's income, and own only one percent of the means of production.[14]

Women should have an input in decision-making about overall project objectives, be included directly as participants in the planning and implementation of development projects, and be seen as beneficiaries of project activities. Development needs to address all spheres of development including the needs of women within their own social, political, environmental and cultural contexts. Women need to be seen as having the role of producers, carers and reproducers, all being essential for the maintenance of the family and community system.

3. GAVVA VILLAGE AND COMMUNITY DEVELOPMENT

Gavva village is a community in the east of Gwoza Local Government Area of Borno State. The village has poor road network and water. This is a complaint made by the villagers to the State Governor, "We are in a critical condition due to lack of motor able road, the problem has negatively affected our socio-economic activities, because we are finding it difficult to convey sick persons and pregnant women on labour to hospital due to inadequate commercial vehicles. Our wives don't attend anti-natal care, secondly we can't convey our farm produce to markets, and government should please save our lives."[15] In addition to that, besides poor road, the area was lacking almost all basic infrastructures, saying during campaigns in previous elections, politicians made several promises to improve their well being but till now there was nothing to write home about.

---

[14] Mosse, 1993.

[15] SUNDAY, 30 AUGUST 2009 Gavva villagers appeal to Sheriff Sunday Trust magazine - Kanem Trust.

The villagers stated that they have presented their problems to Gwoza local government, but was told that the council lacked financial capacity to execute the project. "We are calling on the state government to realize that we are suffering and the situation supposed is not to be so since we are aware that other parts of the state have benefited a lot from developmental projects."[16]

The problem faced by Gavva villagers was alleviated by Basel Mission. The Basel Mission was ready for mission work they eventually in 1957 sent a fact finding group to examine the possibility of entering into the new area, and to view the situation and visit the then Northern Cameroons. They were told by resident officer of the Gwoza area to go to Gavva, where no missionaries had ever been placed before. "At that time, many tribal and clan fights and wars took place in the area. In fact, the plot of land where the missionary station was planned to be built was known as the battlefield of the villages in Gavva area".[17] The talks with the representatives of the government, still under British colonial rule took place. "From the responsible officer it is said that how can there be peace if no peace initiative is being taken like proclaiming the gospel".[18] As a result Basel Mission got permission to start missionary work at Gavva in the so called unsettled region and closed area. As a condition to start missionary work there, it was agreed upon that Basel Mission start doing medical work and open primary schools to educate the children. Consequently, preparations were made to start work. This developmental work done by the Basel Mission was the key factor that helps Gavva area today.

---

[16] SUNDAY, 30 AUGUST 2009 Gavva villagers appeal to Sheriff Sunday Trust magazine - Kanem Trust

[17] Schyett, 2008:18. This was taken from notes sent to Rev.Dauda A.Gava in UKZN South Africa.

[18] Schyett 2008:20. This was taken from notes sent to Rev.Dauda A.Gava in UKZN South Africa.

When one visits Gavva today, the roads built by the Basel mission(aries) in the 1960 are still the ones being used. The pipe water running from the hills provided by the missionaries is still the one used by the people in that area with the exception of few wells that were dug by the Well-Digging project of the Church. This tells how the area has been neglected by both the Church and the Government. It means if our missionaries from Basel did not construct the road and provided water for us, we would not have known our position today. One could see that in those days that people did not hear the Gospel and there were no hospitals, many have suffered. It was good that the missionaries came at that time to save our people from dying. Today, our people still enjoy the hospital built by the missionaries though it has been taken over by the Government. If the hospital were still with the missionaries I believe that it would be more than it is.

I have been to Gavva several times and have seen how the community came together doing communal work to save the road from being unmotor able. The community also dug some wells in order to get water for drinking and other usage. In all this work that has been done women were not left behind. In fact, during all these communal work by the villagers' women participated fully. Apart from participating in the work, they were left with responsibilities of preparing meals and provision of drinking water for hundreds that did the work. Since most of the men today go out in search for jobs to do in the farms or urban areas, women are the ones left with day to day running of their homes. During harvest time, one could see that most of the men would not be at home. The women are left to harvest the corns and do communal work in order to thresh the corn. Many women are involved in sewing and knitting today. They have learned this vocation through the training they received through the EYN women centre, by individual self-employed women and EYN Literacy programme which was initiated by the Basel Mission. this vocation helps the community in economic empowerment because it provides job opportunity to women in the area. I personaly have trained many women in sewing and knitting and these women are empwered today so that they do not have to depend on their spouse completely for financial assistance.

Now in such a situation, it is difficult for a community to develop without the assistance from the government or Non governmental organizations. But unfortunately neither the government nor the non governmental organizations come to the aid of the community. Because of this neglect by the government the villagers are poor roving in a life of poverty. Poverty does not bring development to a community but destroys it. The youth have not gone to school; it means that they are still backward in terms of western education. If they are not educated it would be difficult for jobs to be offered to them except the few that have had their early education in the schools opened by the Basel Mission in the area. Many people were converted to the Christian Faith because of the mission work. From the missionaries, people discovered the love of God in Christ and the ministry of the church today. The teachings in Sunday school, the readings and writings were the beginning of education in the area. This helped in giving enlightenment to the people which was enjoyed by the Basel Mission area of Gavva.

In the work done by the Basel Missionaries at Gavva many women were involved especially in the health sector. And it is known today that health is wealth. It is only the Bible that can bring consolation to communities like Gavva that is neglected by the government.

4. THE BIBLICAL POSITION FOR HELPING THE POOR IN A COMMUNITY

The ethics of generosity in helping the poor is rooted in the person and work of Christ himself according to 2 Cor. 8:9, "For you know the grace of our Lord Jesus Christ, that though He was rich, yet for your sake He became poor, that you through His poverty might become rich." This example of Christ's should lead us to see our responsibility to use the wealth God has entrusted to us to glorify him by sharing with the poor and with a neglected community.

The government and the church should devote the resources to projects that effect permanent socio-economic as well as spiritual change and life of the people. The government should provide the amenities that are necessary for sustenance of life and to impact families and communities with money, help, and the gospel. Many social problems have spiritual and moral causes which need to be addressed at the same time that will meet immediate need.

As Jesus said in Mark 7:14, "The poor will be with you always." It is the government and church's mission not only to fulfil the needs of its own citizens, but to reach out to the rest of the neighbourhood and block. Christ wasn't put on this earth to walk around and be fed spiritually from others. He was here to serve as an example of what a Christian should strive to be- not only living a pure and holy life but to help those in need. Matthew 20:28 says "just as the Son of Man did not come to be served but to serve, and to give his life a ransom for many." Not only does God call us to serve, but he calls us to serve the poor. This is a group of people who are routinely cast aside in life, even by Christians. They are looked at as a problem that needs solving and charity and not as a group of people who need love and care. It is almost as if the poor in our town are not looked at as real people, but rather as "cases". God commands us in Proverbs 31:8 to "Speak up for those who cannot speak for themselves, for the rights of all who are destitute." He has blessed us with the comforts of life and in return asks us to help others who are not so lucky. 1 John 3:17 says "If anyone has material possessions and sees his brother in need but has no pity on him, how can the love of God be in him?"

V. CONCLUSION

It is obvious that women have contributed a lot toward community development in Gavva area. Women were also part of the work done by the Basel Mission Gavva. Though, it seems like men take the glory for the work done by women in the area, this is happening because women were relegated to the background. It would be appropriate for the women to stand on their feet to show that they have and are still contributing a lot to the society not Gavva area alone.

There should be efforts to promote, encourage, and support local level interaction done by women and men as well. Priority should be given to actively pursue community development. A basis for community and economic development can be established in order to help the disadvantaged communities and this would go at great length to help and would alleviate the problems faced by both men and women. Community interaction is most important component in creating awareness, identifying opportunities to positively contribute, and fostering community action. Through these, more comprehensive programs and planning can be conducted and local decision making enhanced. All contribute to local well-being and enhance local quality of life for our communities for development. Church leaders, members and the general community will all take pleasure in development in order to build up community.

BIBLIOGRAPHY

Boserup, E. (1986) *Women's Role in Economic Development.* Gower, Aldershot.

Development Forum (1978) In J.L. Evans, The Intersecting Needs of Women and Children. *Community Development Journal,* vol 20, no. 3, 1985.

Development in Nigeria" in Onakala et al (eds). Environment and Poverty in Nigeria, JAMOE Ent., Enugu.

Evans, J. L. (1985) The Intersecting Needs of Women and Children. *Community Development Journal.* vol 20, no. 3.

Huizer G. (1983) "The Role of Peasant Women's Organizations in Rural Development Case Study of Women's Participation in Co-operative in Zambia"in SID Innovative Approaches to Rural Development, Report of Policy Dialogue held in Rome.

Huntington S. (1975) "Issues in Women's Role in Economic Development: Critique And Alternatves" Journal of Marriage and Family,37, No 1, 4.

Ijere M. (1992) Leading Issue in Rural Development Acena Publishers, Enugu.

Gabriel, T. (1991) *The Human Factor in Rural Development.* Belhaven Press, London and New York.

George, S. (1985) *Ill fares the land. Essays on food hunger and Power.* Writers and Readers, London.

Isbeter, J. (1993) *Promises not Kept : The betrayal of social change in the third world, 2nd edition.* Kumarian Press, Connecticut.

Kihoro, W. (1992) Now, Listen to me! *New Internationalist,* January.

Lee, P. (1993) Women in development : Policy challenges for NGO's. *Development Bulletin.* vol 26, January, 1993.

Lovel, H. and Feuerstein, M. (1985) Women, Poverty and Community Development in the Third World. Editorial. *Community Development Journal,* vol 20, no.3.

Luloff, A.E., and J. Bridger. 2003. "Community Agency and Local Development." Pp. 203-213 in,

Challenges for Rural America in the Twenty-First Century, edited by D. Brown and L. Swanson.

University Park, PA: Pennsylvania State University Press.

Luloff, A. E. and L. Swanson. 1995. "Community Agency and Disaffection: Enhancing

Collective Resources." Pp. 351-372 in *Investing in People: The Human Capital Needs of Rural America,*edited by L. Beaulieu and D. Mulkey. Boulder, CO:Westview Press.

Madu I. (2003) "Participatory Community Driven Action Programme for Sustainable Coastal

March, C., Smyth, I. And Mukhopadhyay (1999) A Guide to Gender-Analysis Frameworks. An Oxfam Publication, London.

Moser, C. (1991) In H. Hill, Looking back - moving forward : AIDAB's review of WID practice. *Development Bulletin,* vol 26, 1993.

Moser, C. (1991) Gender Planning in the Third World : Meeting Practical and Strategic Gender Needs'. In T. Wallace and C. March (eds) *Changing Perceptions: Writings on Gender and Development.* Oxfam, Oxford.

Mosse, J.C. (1993) *Half the World, Half a Chance: An Introduction to Gender and Development.* Oxfam, Oxford.

Narayan D. (1998) "Participatory Rural Development " in Lutz E. et al (eds) "Agriculture and the Environment: Perspectives on Sustainable Rural Development" A World Bank Symposium. The World Bank, Washington D. C.

Okoli F. (1998) "The Relative Position of Women in Contemporary Nigeria," Journal Of Liberal Studies, Cape Publishers International Ltd, Onitsha.

Oji G. (2000) "Determinants of Women Empowerment for Participatory Democracy:Nigeria in Perspective" International Journal of Social Sciences and Public Policy 3 No 2.

Ostergaard, L. (1992) *Gender and Development : A practical guide.* Routledge, London.

Prices, S. (1993) Politics and Practice of Gender Analysis in Development. *Development Bulletin*, vol 26, January 1993.

Staudt, K. (1983) *Women in developing countries: A Policy focus.* The Haworth Press, New York.

SUNDAY, 30 AUGUST 2009 Gavva villagers appeal to Sheriff Sunday Trust magazine - Kanem Trust

Wilhelm, Schett, Notes to Rev. Dauda Andrawus Gava in July 2008.

Wilkinson, K. 1991. *The Community in Rural America.* New York, NY: Greenwood Press.

World Bank (2000) "Attacking Poverty, World Development Report, 2000/2001" The World Bank, Washington DC

The Role of Women in Economic Development of the Church and the Society[1]

Rebecca Samuel Dali

INTRODUCTION

Since the beginning of man's history, man has suffered from his own greed and inability to obey God. Even in the Garden of Eden, Adam and Eve disobeyed God and were cast out to earn their living in their own way. In Genesis 3:19. God says, "By the sweat of your face, you shall eat bread". From that day until Christ returns again, man will continue to be concerned with the challenges of acquiring and managing possessions.

It would be accurate to say that most individual tensions; family frictions, strives, anger and frustrations are caused directly or indirectly by money. Over 85% of the working days for the average individual, are spent thinking about, talking about and in pursuit of money. This area is of great importance to God. It is of such importance that the Bible has hundreds of scripture verses dealing with how to handle money or particularly, the word wealth which occurs more than 240 times in Old Testament.

---

[1] Most of this Article is taken from my book, Rebecca Samuel Dali, Wealth Creation and Savings: Some Biblical Principles and Ethics, (Bukuru: African Christian Textbooks), 2007.

The common statement that says, "Money is easy to spend but hard to get," is a fact. We get money either as a worker or from our businesses but it disappear from our hands faster than we realize it. As such, many Christians today are in deep financial problem. This is evident in the fact that many people complain of their present indebtedness and low wages. In fact, some have become bankrupt: some people are ejected by their landlords because, for months, they have not paid their house rents. This is true in a situation where every month their expenditure exceeds their income. Nothing puts more pressure on marriage than financial irresponsibility, lack of money, and huge debts.

It is not without some basis that women throughout history considered that society dismissed them as second-class citizens, or non-entities, or just being there for man's bidding. During economic hardships, some husband blame their wives for mismanagement. Some say the Bible conveys the same message and is anti-women. Many women felt there are no roles to play in such conditions. It is true that some societies and churches today still keep their women virtually chained to the home. Women are some times abused and oppressed by the harsh and barbaric rule of selfish male-dominated regimes, often in the name of a particular religion or God. But this is not what God ordained for men and women.

Women in the Bible like Esther developed her people spiritually and economically she saved their entire lives from destructions of lives and properties, although with humble beginning as an orphan she was God fearing, humble, obedience and she become a woman of influence dignified by both pagans and her own people. Because Esther fears God, she put God first in everything she does (Esther 3: 16). Not only when pushed by Mordecai in Chapter 4:4, she risks her life and went against the law, "l will go to the King, even it is against the law. And if l perish, l perish." She was courageous, woman of faith full with determination to work for his people to be godly and to face their challenges together.

Christ our Saviour gives us freedom to play our roles freely; Women certainly were close to Christ. They followed Christ to Galilee and Jerusalem. They were there at his crucifixion and were the first witnesses of his resurrection and declared it to the Apostles. Just like all individuals in the Church of God, women too need to be able to give an answer of the hope that lies within them (1Pet. 3:15). As Lydia, Dorcas a lot of wealthy women helped the Apostles and members of the church with their wealth (Acts: 16:13-15)

A lot of women have been blessed and are no longer under this yoke. However history reveals that you cannot be influential without economic power. Poverty hinders many women from performing their roles in both the society and the church.

ROLE OF WOMEN IN ECONOMIC DEVELOPMENT OF THE CHURCH AND THE SOCIETY

BIBLICAL BASIS FOR ECONOMIC DEVELOPMENT

Old Testament and Economic Development

For Christians seeking God's best about wealth, He has established simple, basic principles in the Bible for the management of such, and if we follow God's principles, we will experience peace. (Haggai 2:8, 1 Chronicles 29:12). In spite of the very effort made by anyone to acquire temporary title to God's material gift, it is still God that donates to him. (Deut. 8:18).

Developing economically can be described as strength, might or material prosperity which is the riches that makes persons significant in the society. Joseph in Genesis 45:11 comforted his brothers. Hezekiah had very great riches and honor for God had given him very great possessions. (2 Chron. 32:37, Job 1:3-29, 12-17, Ruth 2:1, 8-9). Abraham, David and others, had possessions.

They have been described as having riches and treasures which indicate their possessions have increased in size and importance. So these people have great supplies of goods to make life easy (Neh. 5:19-19). Melchizedek also blessed Abraham and Abraham was rich (Gen. 14: 19-20).

But there is another theme that runs through the Old Testament; along with the riches are the Lord's blessings for the righteous. Deuteronomy warns of a time when Israel's heart might become proud. "When the day of riches comes, then your heart will become proud and you will forget the Lord your God." (Deut. 8:14). [2]

---

[2] From verses 17-18 it continues "you may say to yourself, 'my power and the strength of my hands have produced this wealth for me. ' But remember the Lord your God, for it is He who gives you the ability to produce wealth, and so confirm His covenant." So in this sense, wealth is a blessing from God, but wealth is also a danger.It can rob a person of humility and sensitivity to the Lord. Developing economically and become Wealthy also has disadvantages because passion for wealth can lead a person into sin. "Wealth cannot endure; neither can it redeem your soul" (Hos. 12:8).

The Psalmist also puts it thus: "But man despite his riches, does not endure" (Ps. 49:6-9). Again he said, we should not envy those who are rich, because, "A man who has riches without understanding is like the beast that perishes (Ps. 49:16-20).

Riches as seen by David are disaster if "the man who is rich did not make God his stronghold but trusted in his great wealth and grew strong by destroying others." (Ps.52:5-7). So it is important reason for us to know that to create wealth or being rich without God is dangerous. We have to trust in God and know that wealth is neither an unmixed blessing nor a guaranteed prospect for the godly. In the framework of the covenant, God's people can expect blessings and this will often take the form of riches.

But Christian riches are never to be idolized (Ps. 10:2-15; 16:21-22). David, Abraham, Joseph, Job etc did not put their trust in their wealth. (Job 31:24-28).

New Testament and Economic Development

Jesus taught about wealth frequently, but the primary focus was on attitude. In Matthew 6:5-34, Jesus taught His disciples how to pray, "…Give us today our daily bread" (vs. 11). Some are of the view that God is against creation, accumulation of wealth and economic development because of some passages in the Bible.

"Do not lay up for yourselves treasures on earth" (Mt. 6:19). Is this admonition against acquisition of wealth? It is then, if the purpose is for saying! But our wealth is not for our soul alone but to be use according to God's purpose.[3] Many people believe that Christians should not have treasures on earth because "money is the root of all evil." They misquote 1 Tim 6:10. "For the love of money is the root of all evil, and some by longing for it have wandered away from the faith, and pierced themselves with many a pang." This is God's perspective; the love of money is the root of all sort of evil.[4]

But another thing that puzzles people today and also the disciples then was astonished is the statement. "Truly 1 says to

---

[3] Because of this verse, some are saying to be wealthy is sin. Having money is not sin! As a matter of fact, many times, when God finds someone with proper attitude, He blesses them with great wealth. When Solomon prayed for wisdom to be able to manage the people of Israel, God responded by granting him wisdom and great wealth.

[4] Christ relates this attitude to the rich young ruler. He came before Jesus and asked Him in Luke 18:18-22, how he should obtain eternal life. Christ told him to obey the commandant of God, which he said he had been observing from his youth. Jesus told him "one thing you still lack, sell all that you possess, and distribute it to the poor, and you shall have treasures in heaven; and come follow me" (v. 22). A lot of people are saying, can only the poor follow Him? And is this a mandate laid on the rich! To go sell what you possess and give it to the poor? It would be recklessly simplistic to so interpret the story. Zacchaeus was not required to do that. He was the one who declared: "Behold, the half of my goods I will give to the poor" (Lk. 19:8).

you, it will be hard for a rich man to enter the kingdom of heaven. Again I tell you, it is easier for a camel to go through an eye of a needle than for a rich man to enter the kingdom of God" (Mt. 19:25-26). Entrance into heaven is quite clear irrespective of wealth. It is by faith, obedience and also a gift of God. "With men, this is impossible but with God all things are possible" (Mt. 19:26). That is, only God can make the dead soul, live and change the alien into a true citizen of the kingdom.[5]

No generalization can be derived from this text. Clearly the Lord dealt then as His word does today, uniquely, with individual who comes seeking direction for the use of his/her wealth. "Instruct those who are rich in this present world not to be conceited or fix their hope on the uncertainty of the riches, but on God, who richly supplies us with all things to enjoy" (1 Tim. 6:17). This passage implies that God is the donor of the riches. "But if anyone of you has the world's goods and sees his brother in need, yet closes his heart against him how does God's love abide in him (1 Jn. 3:17). So we should help the poor and propagate the gospel with our money.

---

[5] The temptations of wealth do indeed threaten entrance into kingdom of God. Neither the abundance nor the absence of riches as such, governs eternal destiny. The soul passes through the eye of the needle by grace, not by selling all that he has. Jesus observed the attitude of the man that he loved money. The young man turned sadly and went away for he was very rich (Lk 18:23). Christ knew that this man loved his money. He has kept all the external commandants, but he could not keep that internal attitude, straight. Because of this, Christ asked him to sell what he has and follow Him. He refused to do so, yet, in death he must surrendered what in life he could not. God is always concerned with our attitudes. Christ's statement dealing with the rich young ruler was based on that man's attitude, his motivation and the purpose behind his money. He was sad; so money does not bring happiness as some Christian's claim. There is no relationship between money and happiness.

No generalization should be made by a simplistic exegesis of selected text. There is nothing wrong in getting money and saving it, Joseph of Arimathea was a rich man (Mt. 27:57), who fulfilled a prophecy (Is. 15:53-59) because his riches gave him access to Pilate to secure the body of Jesus for burial in his new-hewn tomb. Jesus Himself and His disciples were supported by those "who provided for them out of their means" (Lk. 8:3), and Paul was befriended by the wealthy on his journeys (Acts 16:40). Abraham and all the patriarchs were very rich and companions of God. King David was both rich and the prototype of Jesus. Some of Jesus' disciples were reasonably well-to-do (Mk. 1:20) and Jesus had some fairly wealthy friends (Jn. 12:3). He and the twelve disciples shared a common purse (Jn. 12:6). Although they were content to go without the comforts of the home life (Lk. 9:5-8), they saved and give to the poor (Jn. 13:29).[6]

The passages analyzed above shows that nothing hinders us from creating and accumulating wealth.

He cautioned His disciples not to store up treasures on earth; because if people's thoughts and motives are focused on their treasures they will lose sight of Jesus. We can focus on Christ's righteousness and His kingdom and leave it to Him to supply our needs. (Mt. 6:25-34).

Generally, the Bible is saying that riches are blessings if it is used to serve God (1 Tim. 6:18). But riches can be a curse and can lead to destruction and oppression of others. The rich should not oppress the poor (Jas. 5:1-6). Jesus and Apostle Paul's attitude towards money as revealed in the scripture provide us with examples of a contentment that can be applicable in our life circumstances (Phil. 4).

---

[6] Dekoster Berghoef, Deacons Handbook, (Grand Rapids: Christian Library Press), 1980. 38.

Pay God First (Paying Tithe) to Develop Economically

Tithe is giving God the first part of your income as a testimony of His ownership. (Luke 6:38) It is through sharing that we bring God's power in finances into focus. It includes all your lifetime, talents and energy (Mt. 6:19-21, Lk. 12:15, 19-21, 1 Tim. 6:6-11, Prov. 11:24, 25, Lk. 6:38, 2 Cor. 9:8, Is. 58:10, 11).

A lot of Christians have financial difficulty because they are not trusting God as owner of their lives. They have the tendency to want to withhold a part of what they have. They are not faithful in paying their tithes. But until a Christian has experienced freedom in the area of money, he will never experience God's total plan for his life.

Every Christian should establish tithe as the minimum testimony to God's ownership. God want us to give the first part to Him. It is through sharing with Him that we bring His power in finances into focus. Pay your tithes before making any purchases, regardless of the amount. One of the greatest joys that a Christian can experience is God's Faithfulness. Psalms 37:7 says, "Rest in the Lord and wait patiently for him."[7]

---

[7] The correct attitude Christians should have towards wealth is to seek God's purpose for what is supplied to him or her. We have to commit our entire resources to Him. Every thing including money is temporary. The importance of money to God is that he wants to use it to help determine our usefulness to Him throughout eternity. Our commitment to God's word on this earth should be proportionate to our use of money (2 Peter 3:11).

Money is a training ground for God to develop us and for us to discover our trust and worthiness. Jesus says in (Lk. 16:11). "If therefore you have not been faithful in the use of unrighteo mammon (money), who will entrust the true riches to you"? So also Proverbs 3:5-9 says we have to "Trust in the Lord with all your heart and lean not on your own understanding..." and "...Honor the Lord with your wealth, with the first fruits of your crops." We must depend on God totally, because God will do the best for us. (Ps. 50:10-12, 1 Cor. 6:19-20, 1 Chron. 29:11-14). (1 Chron. 27:25).

Just as a Christian cannot experience the fullness of the Holy Spirit until he surrenders ownership of his life to Christ, so too, he cannot experience peace in the areas of finances until he has surrendered total control of this area to God and accepted his position as a steward.[8]

Develop Winning Spirit to Develop Economically

Becoming wealthy and Economic development begins in your brain, not your bank account. If you are thinking about building wealth, an investment strategy, or even if you are simply setting your financial goals, you have already made an important step, starting this process sooner rather than later may well be one of the most important decisions you will ever make.

Wealth and achievements do not come from what we do alone but from who we are. Our worldly power results from our personal power. Our career and wealth is an extension of our personality. Personal power emanates from someone who takes life seriously. The universe takes us as seriously as we take it.[9]

To develop the society and the church economically you must acquire winning spirit, some people said there are seven habits of success, and some say two and others say ten. But Brain Sher, the author of *What Rich People Know and Desperately Want to Keep Secret*, through serious research and working with rich people

---

[8] Michelle Buckingham and Roberts Strand affirm the importance of tithe when they gave three true life story of one man, who tithes faithfully, See Wealth Creation on this subject.

[9] I agree with Marianne Williamson in her book, A Return to Love who comments on personal power. In her words, "Seeing your strength exactly as they are, and equally aware of where they can be best applied, for what, to whom and when, He chooses and accepts your part for you."Marianne Williamson, A Return to Love, (New York: Harper Perennial), 1992, 179.

discover thirty-six personal qualities or as he call it "Your Personal Foundation to Riches."[10]

Save to Develop Economically

Most people who have a net worth of 1 million savings or more started out with very ordinary incomes, so what did they do differently than the rest of us? They all learned to save money on a regular basis, make sacrifices when possible and scrutinize their purchases based on whether they needed the items or simply wanted them. For these individuals, financial independance is more important than displaying their status through expensive possessions.

It is not so much what you earn but what you keep. You have to save 10% and invest it regularly. That will determine your financial success.

Spend Money Wisely to Develop Economically

Budget is very important, what you have left over after your tithe and paying yourself you have to set aside some percentage for primary emergencies. Cut your traveling; if it is not necessary don't travel and save money. Running a motor vehicle could be another major drain on your pocket. Food budgets can sometimes be reduced by up to 25%.

Medical bills can be reduced drastically. Learn basic primary health care and keep your family in general good health. Always have first aid at hand and travel with basic medication. Handsets, be careful on how to use it, call people where it only necessary. Calculate how much you spent in a month then be wise you.

---

[10] Brain Sher, What Rich People Know and Desperately Want to Keep Secret, (Roseville: Prima), 2000, 38. To have full explanations on these principles see my Book Wealth Creation and Savings: Some Biblical Principles and Ethics, 56ff.

By changing your spending and saving behaviors, you will be on your way to a wealthier you. To save entails that you are to reduce your consumption or increase income or doing both. If you do not make sacrifices when possible and scrutinize your purchases based on whether you needed the items or simply wanted them as stated above, you will be indebted and carrying large amounts of debts at high interest rate. This can seriously sabotage your savings plans. If you are looking to start investing but don't quite know where to start, the best thing may be to simply get an understanding of your finances by creating a budget, next seek financial advice.[11]

Invest Wisely to Develop Economically

Improve your skills. If you are a housewife learn something new, e.g. baking, hairdressing, tailoring etc and make it in a special way that people will be attracted to it and buy. You can invest in Shares in companies and banks. Entrepreneurship (setting up your own business) is good and better not to join business with anyone. Money is plentiful if you keep the rules of its acquisitions. There is also good to invest in banks for more than seven years to enjoy the power of compound interest. So do everything possible to increase your earnings and what will make you to save a lot of money.

In our economy today, wealth is still related to money, but the position one holds is also a measure of wealth. Education is also wealth, professional men such as doctors, attorneys, dentists and others are thought to be "wealthy" because of their income-earning potential. A doctor, for example, coming right out of residency, is capable of borrowing great amounts of money to go into business without any collateral other than his education. His credit worthiness is based on his potential productivity. Therefore, even the talents and the abilities that we have are part

---

[11] *Ibid.*

of wealth. "It is the blessing of the Lord that makes rich, and he adds no sorrow to it!! (Prov. 10:22).

Women should encourage the people to share their wealth. Christian creates wealth because it can be used to spread God's word, build hospitals and churches, feed the poor, take care of the widows and orphans (1 Tim. 5:3). God also requires that we provide for our families. (1 Tim. 5:8-16). This admonition from Paul tells us to support the members of our family. So that our family members who are widows; will not be a burden to the church. God also requires every Christian to supply, the needs of those ministering God's words like (pastors, reverends, evangelist, missionaries etc). We are to send them out like respected God's ambassadors, not as people who are poverty stricken. (1 Cor. 9:9-14) "And they bear witness to your love before the church and you will do well to send them on their way in a manner worthy of God. For they went out for the sake of the name accepting nothing from the Gentiles," (2 John 6, 7).

Christians are admonished by God to accept nothing from non-believers but because of poverty Christian or churches are accepting money from non-Christians sources. Also there are five things we can do with money; We need money to give to God tithe; We can spend it; We can save for future needs; We can pay off our debts (if we have any); you can pay your taxes:[12] So if we do not create wealth, where we can get money to tithe, spend and pay for taxes and debts? A person cannot accumulate wealth without saving. We can save through forming associations or through banks and investments.

Stop Getting into Debt to Develop Economically

Debt is an enemy to wealth creation, so don't get into it. Reasons why people get into debts and how to avoid it. Some cannot pay

---

[12] H. B. London and Neil. B. Wiseman, Pastors at Risk, (Wheaton: Victor Book), 1993, 122.

their children school fees, either in primary, secondary or even university, so they end up borrowing to send their children to school. Long range planning should be followed or you can send your children to public or government schools instead of private schools to avoid debts. Some can get into heavy debts because of gambling, lotteries etc. We have already said that this is not included in God's Biblical financial system. Emergency funds is meant for emer-gencies e.g. sickness, death, accident etc, which most experts say you have to save two to six months of your monthly salary.

Why do Christians fall in trap to system of borrowing? As Burkett puts it "they have violated one or more scriptural principles that God laid down particularly those relating to financial bondage."[13] It is important that a Christian under-stands God's attitude about debt. Proverbs 22:7 implies that once someone borrows, he becomes a servant of the lender, and the lender has established an authority over the borrower. When a Christian continues to borrow without the means to repay, his attitude falls into the category of deceit and greed. This mindset will surely separate any Christian from God's will. (Lk. 12:15). That is the danger of borrowing and indebtedness, but God wants Christians to be debt free we should deal with and get out of debts.

CONCLUSION

Let me warns all of us that there is misery to develops economically without Christ, wealth without Christ is vanity. A lot of wealthy people are worried, frustrated and upset about money. But God will never use money in a Christian life to worry him. If you are worried about money it is an absolute certainty that God is not in control. Remember, God said that wealth without worry is His plan for our lives. So if we are worried and

---

[13] Burkett, *op.cit.*, 68.

upset over abundance or lack of money God is not managing our affairs (Mt. 6:25). God will supply our needs.

A lot of Christians are being corrupt with money. Many Christians have fallen into Satan's trap and are being corrupted. They fail to realize this principle; God cannot be in control when they are becoming corrupt (Ps. 1:6). A Christian whose financial life is characterized by greed, ego, deceit or any of the many other worldly snares is not God's allay.

Frequently, Christians are trapped by financial ego. Most people cater to the wealthy in our country. Too often in our churches the deacons are selected because of their wealth or position rather than by their spiritual commitment to the Lord. It is important to understand, God will not use money to build our egos. In Christ we are all financially equal. The things of this world will quickly pass away. Death will remove all wealth from us, and when we (as Christians) meet again, there are going to be many surprises. Those who will have the crowns of heaven and are placed in charge of the cities of God will not be those using money to build egos (Jas. 1:10, 11; Ps. 49:10, 11; Rev. 3:18). That is why wealth without Christ is misery. Example of some people who developed economically without Christ thus;

In 1923, an important meeting took place in Chicago. Nine of the most financially successful people in the world attended. It was a gathering of people who knew the secrets of making money, and lot of it. Where were they in 1948, 25 years later?

- The world greatest wheat speculator died abroad insolvent.

- The president of the world's largest independent Steel Company died in bankruptcy after living on borrowed money for the precious five years.

- The president of the largest Utility Company became a fugitive from justice and died a pauper in a foreign country.

- The member of the president cabinet was pardoned from prison sentence and died penniless at home.

- The president of the New York stock Exchange ended up in prison.

- The president of a Gas Company was declared insane.[14]

- The other three men remained wealthy and genuinely prosperous, as have many of history's happiest and most successful people who have pursued prosperity and not simply material wealth. They listen to God and read His word to learn how to manage all that has been given to them according to the principles, values, motives and priorities of the highest source of truth.

Those six men knew how to make a lot of money, but they failed to truly prosper. Those people were without Christ and they depended on their wealth. Proverbs 23:4, 5 caution us, "Don't worry yourself to gain riches, cease from your consideration of it! When you set your eyes on it; it is gone. Wealth certainly makes itself wings like an eagle that flies toward the heavens." Really, these 6 wealthy people lost every-thing because their eagles flew away. This is because they did not put their trust in God, but in their wealth.

There is nothing that compares to the promise and hope of a life lived in a partnership with God. May the Lord help us to serve him faithfully, may He provide our needs according to his purpose and glory. Amen

---

[14] Strand, *op.cit.*, 82.

The Church's Role in Empowering Women for Effective Ministry

Roseline Luka Vandi

INTRODUCTION

In this study, the researcher has observed that, there is a high rate of negligence of women empowerment by some churches due to their church politics. This has led Christ women into full time business of their own rather than concentrating on church activities.

Another issue that the researcher observed is that, the God given gifts in women has been neglected. Hence the church is not supposed to be what it is meant for. But in Genesis 2:18-25, God gave woman responsibility as a help mate for the man which suggested the possibility for a woman to work with the man. Women have potentials that can be explored but, "have been neglected by the church. Some of our churches do not allow women to explore their potentials so as to assist the church.

Similarly, the research seeks to draw the attention of church leaders to see women as co-workers in the vineyard of God. With this understanding we will be considered as God's children and members in one big family of God.

In spite of the challenges we have ahead on the thought as to what the church can do to empower women for effective ministry, we cannot run away from the fact that women, right from time have been relegated to the background to be seen as second class creatures. In view of this, this paper seeks to proffer solutions on what the church can do to empower women for effective ministry in the church.

1. DEFINITION OF TERMS

1.1 Role

The Random House Dictionary defines role "as the part or character that an actor present in a play in its proper or customary function."[1] But the researcher looked at role as" a person who played a part being assigned or is a specific task or function given to a person to play".

1.2   Empowering

Empowering in the context of this paper, is not all about Women's ordination and exercising authority over men. But rather, women empowerment is viewed in terms of ensuring responsibilities in the activities of the church. It is also to help women to demonstrate their own God's given gift posterities in the church. It means also ensuring that women are able to participate fully in building the body of Christ in terms of assuring responsibilities such as preaching, teaching, administering e.t.c.

2. LITERATURE REVIEW

2.1 Introduction

This section analyzes a historical appraisal of women's empowerment in African views as presented by other scholars to find out what they have written and the position of the author's. There are many materials written on women's empowerment, which could be reviewed but due to limited space for this paper, the literature cannot all be reviewed. Therefore I found it necessary to review some materials that are relevant to this work particularly published and unpublished materials that direct bearing on the topic.

2.2. African View of Women's Empowerment

The Leadership of women in Africa in the olden days a pretty is not picture. In the traditional societies of Africa women were to be seen in public and not to be heard. Their leadership was neglected and also looked down upon due to the cultural background. Women were only represented by men in all activities in the society. They were discriminated against. They were restricted from participating in sacred rituals they were banned from contributing in any discussion held by the clan, town and village.

The Jews in the days of Jesus treated women as second class citizens. In Corinth women were told not to speak but to be silent in public; like wise most cultures of Africa are treating women as second class citizens. Men do not consider it necessary to consult their wives before taking any important decision that affect the family. And that is why some women are afraid of working face to face with adults, particularly men. It must not be forgotten that we are invited as men and women to seek a new way of being a true church today.

Jane, Gitaued showed disharmony between spiritual and what has been demonstrated since the beginning of time. She affirms women without a doubt are full in the plans and purposes of God. She traced the truth of this to the Jerusalem encounter at Pentecost where men and women were equally equipped to function fully in the body of Christ.

One thing to consider with this author's book is that scholars need to look into some of her interpretation. The author's contribution to this research is important. Like Craig Keener, she gave meaning to some of Paul's text to suit the call for women to be ordained in the church. This may not go well with the traditional view but it is heart warming to some people who have never thought of it that way. Cindy tries to persuade men and women in order to liberate women and persuade them as to God's call on their lives. This will empower women to have more responsibilities in the church and consequently in the society.

"Women in the African church" in the Anitepam Bulletin says the church should focus her attention on empowering women for full participation in all aspects of the church's leadership through the development of skills.[1] She looks at lack of training as the major reason for disregarding women's contribution to the growth of the church. She believes that with the change in the society and the full participation of women in theological education, women can teach, preach, lead and even be ordained in the church today. Therefore she calls upon the church to equip more women with appropriate skills that will be respected and recognized by the community of believers.

Philomena Mwaura in "Empowering of women: the role of the church" describes the recent changes in the society which have resulted from feminist activities. She talks about the plight of the African, whose status has been inferior to that of the man motivated by culture, religious and social bias.[2]

The writers believes that church as the body of Christ, can empower women in areas of life such as education, economics and pastoral work in spite of many hindrances to women's empowerment. Based on this view, the author has given us a logical and clear presentation of women's empowerment, except that religious empowerment has not received the needed attention.

---

[1] Jess Stein (ed.), "Role" The Random House Dictionary of the English Language (New York: Random House publishers nd), 1241.

[2] Jane Gitaured, "Women in the Africa church" The Anite Pam Journal Bulletin November 2002 No 36, 12.

The church needs to start from home if she is really to empower the women.

Women's ministry in the church. An African perspective edited by Alan M. Chilver said that the church should stop addressing women in terms of sons and used the language of Paul when he says "I will be a father to you and you will be my sons and daughters, says the Lord Almighty".[3] (2 Cor. 6:18). The church should encourage women to undertake theological studies granting them equal benefits and then let the church consecrate them into various ministries according to the gifts that the spirit of God has imparted to them.[4] The writer believes that, the Christian life being in grace (Eph 2:5), Christian Ministry is undertaken by grace and through grace (1 Cor 12:4-11) and if ministry in the Church is understood in the sense of service then all areas of ministry in the Church are open to women.

Looking at Chilvers's view, I feel very comfortable with his view because both men and women are servants of God. The scripture made us to understand that your sons and your daughter shall prophesy. Here also women have equal standing with men for proclaiming the gospel of the grace of God to people.

Christian women need to be encouraged to be believed that they too can be meaningful in God's service because Christian men need to discover the comfort and joy of working in equal male-female partnership and because the sin of sexism must be exorcised from the modern Christian community.

---

[3] Philomena Mwaura "Empowering of women: the role of the Church, Journal of African Christian Thought, 1998, vol, 1 No. 1. 28.

[4] Alan M. Chilver (ed.), Women's Ministry in the Church: An African Perspective, (Jos: Theological and Christian Education Commission of the Association of Evangelical in African Nigeria 19927, 11-116

3.   BIBLICAL UNDERSTANDING OF WOMEN EMPOWERMENT

3.1 The Biblical understanding of women's empowerment is very clear. From the creation story one understands that God created man and woman with equal worth and authority (Gen 1:26-27). Neither of them was more equal in God's image and likeness. God gave them equal mandate and dominion to rule and subdue the earth (Gen1:28). God emphasized equality greatly here, He hasn't heard either of them (Adam and Eve) claming superiority. Therefore both the old and New Testament gave a theological basis for women's empowerment.

3.2.   Old Testament View of Women Ministry.

Women ministry in scripture is not a hidden agenda, it is very clear. Although women did not serve as priest in ancient Judaism, but they have played important role in the plans and purposes of God on earth in different capacities that at times gave them authority in both religious and secular matters. Looking through the Old Testament for the women are remarkably[5] prominent for the ministry. They served as Judges, prophetess, queens and those whom God called to perform certain duties.

The first thing that the Bible tells us about is that, women are human beings made, in the image and likeness of God at creation (Gen 1:26). Since every woman is made the image of God, therefore every human being is worthy of honor and respect, whether man or woman. Women are vital instruments that God uses in fulfilling his purpose or plans they respond quickly to God's call for mission.

Herbert says "that in the Old Testament some of the finest leaders in Israel were women, in spite of the fact that the culture was male dominated. Ministry victories were sometimes won because of the courage of women (Judges 4:9ff; Esther 4-7)[6]

---

[5] *Ibid*, 117.

[6] Harbert Lockyer (ed.), "Women" The Illustrated Dictionary, (London: Hodder and Stoughton) 1987, 1105.

As mentioned earlier, women in the Bible served as Judges, queens and prophetess, some of these women can be seen as our examples and their role played in the Old Testament.

DEBORAH

Deborah the wife of Lappidoth was called a prophetess in Judges 4:4 and served as Judges in chapter 4:5 (NIV). She was a mother to Israel and leading Israel. Trust and confidence were already bestowed by on her by the Israelite. They have seen the need for her to be a Judge that is an empowerment, though there were already bestowed on her by the Israelites many men that could have served as Judges she was successful in her works as Judges because we were told in VS 5. That, she held court in the hill country of Ephraim, and both men and women of Israel came to her to settle their disputes. [7] She was a courageous woman as a prophetess and assumed spiritual leadership. As Judges she exercised Judicial and political power she always listened attentively to God's instruction.

She functioned as a civil ruler and was respected for her anointing and spiritual insights and on this basis that she could win the battle. She commanded or instructed Barak son of Abinam on what to do. We found Deborah speaking authoritatively as God's prophetess to Barak in Judges 4:14 (NIV). looking at Deborah as prophetess as well as a Judge and a courageous woman who delivered the Israelites, this is contrary to what some men expect those who regard women as senseless and think that nothing good can come out from their mouth. Nobody can ignore the story of faithful and brave Deborah who spoke the truth as we have heard or seen from the Old Testament.

---

[7] Simon Hodo Abbas, Women on the Pulpit, (Lagos:Soliders of the cross, 2004), 43.

HULDAH

Huldah in the Old Testament most of the prophets were men, when the opportunity was given to Huldah to serve as prophetess she did well. She was empowered by her people and God gave her the approval. The prophetic ministry was the highest gift for religious function in the Old Testament. The prophets have authority to correct and rebuke the priest for their wrong doing and have right to appoint kings. However, Huldah rendered God's word to Josiah who responded quickly to her prophesy (2 kings 22:14-20)[8]

ESTHER AND RUTH

Esther and Ruth have and contributed greatly to the salvation of the Israelites and the entire world through God's leadership in their lives. They saved and delivered the entire nation of Israel.[9] The books of Esther and Ruth are both named after women after who showed that women have played significant roles in ancient Jewish patriarchal society.[10]

Esther is an example of a woman leader in high government position that affected the entire nation. Esther was greatly mentored by mordecai her uncle. The mentoring gave her the ability to serve as queen in a foreign land. Even though she did not served in a place of Ecclesiastical authority, but through her prayer and courage she was able to save and deliver her people by pleading, falling at his feet and weeping. She begged him to put an end to the evil plan of Haman the Agagite (Esther 8:3).

---

[8] Rebecca Samuel Dali, Women in the ministry of Jesus where are they?, (Jos: Anet productions), 2000, 67.

[9] Russel.C. Prow, Women in the Old Testament, (Grand Rapids: Eerdmas pub. Com.) 1951, 66.

[10] Ruth A. Tucker, Women in the Maze. Questions and Answers on Biblical Equality, (Illinois; Intervarsity press), 1992, 65.

MIRIAM

Another example of woman prophetess was Miriam; Miriam Moses' sister was also considered a leader in ancient Israel. Miriam stay with her brothers Moses and Aaron, gave her the ability to be vocal and appreciated God for what He did in their lives. Micah 6:4 says, "I brought you up out of Egypt and redeemed you from the land of slavery. I sent Moses to lead you also Aaron and Miriam" (NIV) based on this verse, she was part of leadership and the one who spoke for and represented the authority of God to people. And this is one of the reasons why she was described as a prophetess in Exodus 15:20. When the Israelites passed through the sea on dry ground, it was Miriam who led women in songs and a choir leader and she took a tambourine in her hand all the women followed her with tambourines and dancing.

Miriam sang to them exalting the name of God Almighty for his deliverance to the Israelites (Exodus 15:1ff). it is also important to mention the effort of Moses's mother to save Moses from pharaoh and pharaoh' his daughter who picked him. More so, Shiprah and Puah, the midwives who feared God and did not do what the King of Egypt told them to do (Exodus 1:15-21).

As earlier mentioned, women have played an important role in the Old Testament. They have become rulers and delivered their people, and whenever they prophesied nobody spoke against them. Women in the Old Testament had freedom and authority. They used their gifts and talent to serve God and their nation it is important to realize that they were never for bidden to speak in public, or to hold leadership positions.

3.2. New Testament View of Women Ministry

The question of the place of women in church's ministry is linked with the question of the status of women generally and their roles in society. In the New Testament, there are evidences that showed that, women did play a role in leadership and ministry in the early church. It is true that while Jesus chose his disciples He chooses only men as members of the twelve disciple women were not among them. But the accounts showed that, women have had a remarkable roles play in the accounts of Jesus' ministry. He was ready to teach them like men (Luke 10:39). He accepted them as person as well spoke to them in the public and also individually.[11] It is very good to start with God's plan of saving mankind and He decided to use a woman to bring forth our savior Jesus. For the fact that God Himself chose Virgin Mary in this special ministry, there is every need for women to be encouraged in the ministry by the church. (Matthew 1:18-25; Luke. 1:1:26-38 NIV).

Jesus himself used the parable of the ten virgins to explain what the kingdom of God will be like in Matthew 25:1-13(NIV). Also in Mark 7:24-30 Jesus performances a miracle of casting out demons from the syrophoenician woman's daughter because of her faith. Jesus also commended the effort or ministry of a woman that anointed him in Bethany (Matt. 26:6-13 NIV). Jesus also commended the widow for her offering in Mark 12:41-44).

In Luke8:1-3 some women who followed Jesus were mentioned, Mary called Magdalene, Joanna the wife of Chuza, Susanna and Many other's. "These women were supporting the ministry of Jesus and the apostles out of their own means" NIV). During the resurrection of Jesus Christ it was women who were the first to witness to, and also were the first to witness to, and also were the first preachers of the resurrection of Jesus Christ.[12] The fact that these women followed Jesus made it possible for them to learn a lot from him by this we could say that Jesus

---

[11] Susan T. Foh, Women and the Word of God. A Response to Bibical feminism, (New Jersey: Presbyterian and Reform Publishing com.), 1976, 91.

[12] A.M MCGrath, Women and the Church, (New York: Darton Longman and Todd Ltd.), 1966, 31.

empowered them. In cenchreae, Paul was referring to her as a patron and benefactor of the church as a whole[13] Rom. 16:1-2).

Phoebe was another example of women who were involved in ministerial work is Lydia. When Paul founded the church in Philippi he involved women in the starting of the synagogue and Lydia became Paul's first convert. Lydia hostel church meetings in her house and probably became the leader of the church. This indicated that women have played a significant role in the Philippians church.[14]

Mary Evans asserts that, "among the four people mentioned by name in the epistle as being workers, two are men and two women. Epahroditus, my brother and fellow worker. Eudodia, syntch and clement were all labored side by side with Paul in the gospel."[15] and some suggest that Euodia and Synthche acted as hostesses for house church in Philippi. Mary the mother of John mark also donated her house as a meeting place in Jerusalem Acts 12:12.

Pricilla and Aguilla were among the noted laborer in the early church. They were in the same business with Paul, as well as shared their lives together they were live in the same room with Paul. They also hosted church meetings in their home.[16] Women were not left behind in the ministry work to save lost soul for Christ in Paul's ministry since the command given to go out to preach the gospel is for everyone crated in God's image whether man or woman.

---

[13] Dacholom Datiri, Lecture note on Paul's Theology and practice of mission MTB 534, (TCNN Bukuru: MTH) 2007, 15.

[14] Mary Evan, Women in the Bible. Esther (London:The Peternoster Press) 1983, 128.

[15] Mary Evan, Women in the Bible, (London: The Peternoster Press) 1983, 128.

[16] Micheal Bruce and G.E Duffield, (ed.) Why not Priesthood and the ministry of women (Abindom; Marcham Manor Press), 1972, 65.

It is clear that after the fall, women took an inferior position because of sin, which had distorted the image of God in them (man and woman), Gen.3:16). But in the New Testament, this inferiority was removed on woman by Jesus Christ Jesus had already wiped out cultural differences between men and women and women in Christian circles. Women experience the saving grace of Golden equal terms with men (Gal 3:28).

The only seemingly controversial statements about women are found in Paul's epistles. Paul says in 1 Cor.14:34, that women should remain silent in churches. They are not allowed to "speak" many people have minister-prated this verse in negative perspectives. But what Paul wanted to point out here is that, he requested women to be submissive to their husbands to preserve order within the church and to be a witness to outsiders."[17] Paul is appealing for order in the church, since God is not a God of disorder but of peace. Peace is found only were there is order. Order is kept when there is law in place. The restriction on speaking should not be taken literally.

In the New Testament, women are often cited as Paul's co-worker. It is good to mention the good works of Dorcas Paul's female assistants which is selfless assistant according to Virgina in her book "women, men and the Bible" [18] Dorcas demonstrated an act of love and charity to the poor.[19]

According to what we have heard from both New and Old Testament women were not hindered from playing any ministerial roles. They also served like Judges, minister, and

---

[17] D. Guthrie, New Bible commentary, (London: Intervarsity Press) 1970, 1070.

[18] Virginia Ramey Mollenkott, Women, men and the Bible, (New York:The crossroad Publishing company 1988), 100.

[19] Arthur G. Patzia, The Emergence of the church context, Growth, Leadership, (Illinois: Intervarsity Press), 2001, 176.

evangelist like Paul. Paul even mentioned some of them as his co-workers.

Therefore, women are special people that God makes use of, in a special way just to shame the foolishness of some ignorant men, who look at women from a cultural perspective. Women are unique human beings because they share equality with men in terms of intellectual, spiritual and emotional standard. However as we proceed in this research we shall look into other challenges of this women's empowerment.

4.   CHALLENGES TO WOMEN EMPOWERMENT TODAY

4.1 Cultural Bias and Prejudice

 Culture is always seen as people's way of life and is has gone a long ways in affecting Christian activities, since it is very difficult to change it. Concerning women's involvement in the ministry, culture is the greatest barrier to them. It has come to surface that culture as observed and maintained by some male. Christian in churches today have contributed to the hindrance to women, participating fully in the evangelistic ministry. For instance, some of the culture in Africa believed that women are weaker creatures. Therefore, they should not talk in public places and have no participation in decision making. Their role is just to cook, bear children in the home and care of household duties. Such culture has affected women in rendering services to God.

Especially in Kamue culture both in behavior and thought and hence excluded in any societal decision taking.[20] They were not expected to talk while men are having conversation. All the hard labors were done by women, faming, planting crops, harvesting, grinding, fetching of fire wood from the bush, cooking etc and there is no appreciation from their husbands. Some call

---

[20] Suzan Mark. "The comparative study of Kamue and Jesus, Attitudes toward women"(Bukuru BD thesis TCNN) 1999, 21.

them cheep laborers and that is why polygamy is so rampant in kamue land. Women are seen as incomplete human being. Such penetrated deeply into the cultural beliefs of some Christian men even among the church leaders (Both ordained and none ordained male ministers of God). As a result of upholding such a negative belief in them, they look down on women as human beings who are not capable to do spiritual ministries. These negative attitudes have resulted to assigning women lesser works or duties in churches to do.

Moreover, it has been observed traditionally that men were and are instrument that God used in bringing development and growth to societies, States and nation of the world at large, but not the women who were and are seen as instrument that God uses only for the progress of the families through child-bearing. To this assertion John Macquarie's also observes that "the assumption operates that, men have been the active agents of historical changes while women provided the stability of cultural continuity, with the domestic household.[21] It has also been noted by Herbert that "most Nigerian men see women as inferior to men, and only useful for producing children and attending to the needs of men."[22] Mission focus added to this by saying that "there are still aspects of the Nigeria law that seem to recognize customary laws which regard women as second class citizens and inferior to men".[23]

It is clear that after the fall, women took an inferior position because of sin, which had distorted the image of God in them

---

[21] John Macquarrie, The Westminster Dictionary of Christian Ethics, (Charlo Hesville: west minister press 1967, 1663.

[22] Herbert Lockyer (ed.), "Women" The Illustrated Bible Dictionary, (London:Hodder and Stoughton, 1987, 1105.

[23] Victor, O. Musa et. al. Wission focus Mobilizing Christian mission, (Jos: Vol 2 May-4 August, 2006, 4.

(man and woman) (Gen 3:16). But in the New Testament, this inferiority was removed on women by Jesus Christ. Jesus had already wiped out cultural differences men and women in Christian circle. Women experience the saving grace of God on having looked at the cultural challenges of women empowerment today; I am saying that, leaders should not maintain culture as their excuse to hinder women empowerment in the church. The Bible should be placed higher than our culture because if opportunities are given to women today in our various churches to demonstrate their potentials, they will make positive development to the church locally and globally.

4.2 Education

Among the numerous factors that affect the effectiveness of women empowerment today is lack of sound and qualitative education. Most of them have not attained any reasonable level of education to enable them to meet the challenges of this day. And this makes them to shy away from responsibilities. Christian knowledge is essential and effective in women's ministry.

4.3 Finance

Another factor that hinders women empowerment today is lack of finance to get into theological education. Some of our churches do not support women with money in order to enable them in their training because our churches today put more effort in building mighty-mighty churches rather than supporting women financially

4.4 Inferiority Complex

Inferiority complex is a feeling that one is less important incapable of doing something. It is obvious that such feeling could either came from women themselves or from the church attitude toward them. They could also feel inferior because the norms of the society create such instincts in them.

Alan M. Chiver says that, "most women shy away in defining who they are (personality). This is as a result of inferiority complex that has been imparted on them right from childhood that they are "less than men, created for me to serve, to obey and to satisfy men's needs."[24]

4.5 Denominational Doctrine

The history of the church reveals that women have been involved in caring mission of the church even when they excluded from the pastoral office. The women's participation in ministry today is some how, most of them are still kept in dependent child like position and not given their own opportunity to develop their skills for self direction today in the church. The scripture talks about God given abilities to individuals for the edification of His church here on earth (1 cor.12:28-31 NIV).

4.6 Male Chauvinism

It is obvious that most African societies and churches are male domineering in terms of decisions making and leadership." The power lies in the hand of men who have the right to speak and take initative to the maintain silence."[25] Chilver says that "Christian men should note that 60% of the congregation are women in many of our churches, but often have no say in thee decisions and policies that affect or concern them in the church. They are silent majority, excluded from any areas of effective service and witness for our lord Jesus, unable to fulfill their calling and responsibilities as equal partners and heirs of the kingdom of God" [26]

---

[24] Alan M. Chilver(ed.), Women's ministry in the Church: An African perspective (Jos: Theological and Christian education commission), 1997, 113.

[25] Mark Hopkins, Lecture note on Global Trends, (TCNN BUKURU:BD) 2002.

[26] Alan M. Chilver (ed.), 115.

Since God has a good plan for mankind and command was given to every on whether man or woman to carry the gospel to the unreached for the growth of the kingdom of God, the church as a whole should address issues that seem to be hindrance along the way of women empowerment for effective ministry. Women suffered for long because of the these factors mentioned above. Some of these could be dealt with if only we know their root causes in our society.

5. CONTEMPORARY WOMEN MINISTRY

The participation of women in the scripture gave raise to the participation of women, have played vital roles in the spread of the gospel. They played the brain behind most of the missionary work and the growth of the church.

Among such example is Sarah major, Hack man assert that, Sarah major was the first

Women preacher among the Brethrens and was considered as a powerful and popular speaker in the annual conference of the church of the Brethren (CBN). She was also active in working among the black people, doing home visitation and working against the use of alcohol. Sarah as popular speaker changed the mind of many men who were opposed to women preaching after they heard her speak. And finally.

Women were given right to be ordained.[27] Norman comments on Bertilla as another example of women who touched the lives of many people through her speech and carefully teaching of religious principles. She taught people how to "Help one another in charitable affection and also to behave purely and be always ready for prayers and take care of the quests and the poor with

---

[27] Galen. R. Hackman "major... preacher "introduction to Brethren History, (Mubi published by TEE college) 1992, 52-53.

concern and to love their neighbors."[28] This woman had highest devotion for the programme of the Church and alters for Christ her activities have influenced many souls and multiplied through the grace of God.

He further states that Mary Webb was another figure who "gathered the fourteen Baptist together and congregational women and organized the Beston Female Society of Missionary purposes which according to Norman the "first feminist movement in North America."[29] He further says that these women's missionary movement grew up rapidly. And the societies were organized and directed by women for the purpose of sending women to the foreign field to evangelize."[30]

Other women were missionary wives for example the wives of Stover Kulp and Albert Helser who came to Nigeria to work with their husbands. They dedicated their interest in the work of mission among Higgi people at Mbororo. They also went to areas that men did not go easily. They collectively played very important roles in evangelism and the growth of the Church among the Kamue people.[31] Women in the West involved in mission throughout the history of the Church, served in different capacities, some of them served as nurses, medical doctors, teachers, ministers and wives of missionaries.

In Africa, the case is not different, today we have leading theologians as Isabel Apawophiri a senior lecturer in the department of theology and religious studies at the University of

---

[28] Nornan E. Thomas (ed.), Classic Texts in Mission and World Christianity. (Maryknoll: Orbis Books publisher),1995, 23.

[29] *Ibid*, 71

[30] *Ibid*, 71

[31] Bitrus A. Bdlia et al, The progressive History of the Ekklesiyar Yan'uwa A Nigeria (EYN), (Jos: Middlend press) 1998, 64.

Malawi, she has served on several levels in the Church and International Committees like circle of concerned African women theologians (CCAWT).

In Nigeria, we have a good number of women who are actively involved in Church ministry. Women like Dr. (Mrs.). Idahosa, Bishop and General overseer of Church of God's mission Nkechi Eneh general overseer of Glorious Church, evangelist Dr. (Mrs.) Agbzue Joy Ifeyinwa is a motivational speaker, educator, counselor, wife and mother. She is the state overseer of world wide flame fellowship on the Hill Evangelical fellowship. Tina D.S Adams who took over the ministry of her husband after his death. We still have many of them that shown us that, if the Church empower women, they will move mountains to the glory of God.

Despite the fact that the Church has been reluctant to empower women for effective ministry, women have contributed greatly to the development, and growth of our Churches today through the following areas.

6.1 Evangelism

Evangelism is a command given to every believer to go out and proclaim the good news of Christ in Matthew 28:18-28. This command was given to both men and women. And because of the importance of evangelism, women consider it as one of their goals. And they are active and still active in doing it and the upliftment of the spirit and moral status of their members.

Women fellowship do gather and tax themselves for the work of evangelism, they also make free will donation, end of month offering to prepare them to go for evangelism. A case study of TEKAN women fellowship go to both near and far places for evangelism such as Koma mountains, Gwoza and malawi areas. They distributed food, clothes, detergent, money etc. For the needy, most women in our various Churches have purchased busses for evangelism which supported the Church as a whole to carry out evangelism. They also do follow up on the young converts and also support the missionaries who are planting Churches in some of the unreached areas.

6.2 Visitation

The women always carry out regular visitation to the bereaved, needy, sick, widows, orphans and the less privileged. They also do hospital and home visitation, helping people in need in kind and cash. They provide fire wood and water to aged in the rural areas and also take care of people who are neglected by their families such as people living with **HIV/AIDS** or Tuberculoses (TB) etc.

6.3 Fund Raising

women also take active part in the financial interest in their local congregations. In most cases they serve as the back-bone of the Church's finances. They donate materials toward their Church building, in ways that shows them as pillars of their congregations. They are indeed serving as, supporting beams of the Church and refuge in times of financial adversity.

6.4 Training of Leaders

Training of Leaders Women have immensely contributed toward the training of leaders, EYN women fellowship every year sends money to help student here in TCNN and in our Bible schools which I believe is one of the means of sustaining students in the cause of their studies

6.5 Leadership Training

Leadership training programmes are organized by the women to educate the leaders of their roles and help them function effectively. During this training, they also organized Bible Quiz competition to test understanding as well as encourage members in studying their Bibles.

7. CHURCH'S ROLE IN EMPOWERING WOMEN FOR EFFECTIVE MINISTRY

It is disheartening to note that some Churches feels very reluctant to confer serious responsibilities on women. This entails corruption of power on the side of women. Their roles are been neglected in the church. As M. Kouzes observes "people who feel Powerless, be their managers or subordinates, tend to hoard whatever sheds of power they have".[32] He further maintains that, "everyone had to feel that they could make a contribution otherwise, they wouldn't count".[33] Bearing this in mind, the researcher is appealing to churches to be concern on what women want and to be sensitive to their needs. For this will enhance the effectiveness of the ministry. The following discourse could be some of the conduct the church needs to employ in order to empower women for effective ministry.

7.1 Planning and Policy

The church should be able to involve and recognized woman's opinions and ideals in planning and policy making in the church. And strife from cultural barriers that seems to militate against. The capabilities of women in social responsibility, for instance, some of the African culture believes that women are weaker creatures. Therefore, they should not talk in public paces and have no participation in decision making. Their role is just to cook, bear children and take care of household duties.

Education

The church should ensure educational resources for good education of woman to enable them in their studies such as

---

[32] James m. Kouzes and Bamy Z. Posner, The leadership challenges, (San Francisco: Jossey-Bass publishers), 1987, 162-163.

[33] Sarah Cunningham (ed.), We Belong together, churches in solidarity with women, (New York: Friendship Press, 1989, 113.

scholarship they should make every effort to equal participation enrolment of woman in theological institution of training and Bible schools because most women are at law level when it comes to the level of education. And educated women in the church also should organize evening class or trading class for those who are doing nothing in their homes and also to ensure that basic knowledge is given to them to empower themselves. Women should make efforts toward their education, especially women fellowship by raising funds to train those that are willing to school and sponsor those that are already in school. They should also motivate rich members to support women training in both secular and theological education.

7.2 Leadership Position

It is quite amazing that there has never been a time when a woman had the president or general secretary of the church. This entails women have not been given their rightful position in the church. If justice will reign woman should be given responsibilities as men for the fact that there have been some men who occupied those leadership positions and were found in efficient, why not try women? Therefore the church should reorganize the leadership positions, which have been exclusively male. Chilver assert that "Christian communities should be educated on scriptural and historical practices that could challenge customs that have consequently led to male dormancy in church leadership. Efforts should therefore be made at all costs to examine and establish a church structure, which gives equal honour and representation to both sexes".[34]

7.3 Adequate featuring of women on the church Rosters

The researcher observed that in some of our churches women are not given a considerable chance to feature on the church rosters

---

[34] Alan, M. Chilver (ed.), Women's ministry, 61.

even though, they are trained, preaching, leading and teaching are not given to them in the adult section in some churches. In regard to this, our churches should feature women on her church roster in order to benefit from the gifts and the potential of women and also to be fully shared in God's comprehensive mission. Preaching and teaching should be given to women in the adult section during morning serve of the church.

7.4 Ordination

Ordination the church should empower women through ordaining those who have Undergone theological education and are sound spiritually, theologically and educationally. Because ordination of women in EYN church is not allowed. Only few among the TEKAN churches allow women ordination. Today there are more than enough women in these churches who are qualified to be ordained like their opposite sex but have been denied by most church traditions. But the question is that, if women can teach or train men to be ordained as pastors, what will hinder their own ordination? And if a woman can do that, there is no need to refuse them ordination if we are to face reality.

7.5 Empowering of Pastor's Wives

Empowering of pastor's wives majority of the indigenous African women look at their husbands call to ministry as their own. Therefore most of them resigned from their job to support their husbands. Yet they came to them as pasters wives. Some lay – women see them as incapable to solve their problems because some churches failed to re define the roles of the pastor's wives in the church some pastor's wives even see themselves in that perspective. Therefore the church should re-define the role of pastor's wives and make space for their full participation in the church programmes as co-workers with their husbands.

7.6 Empowering lay women thought Bible studies

The lay women should be empowered with the knowledge of the Bible. They should be helped to know what the Bible says about themselves as God's image, helping them to know how to read and how to interpret the Bible. The church can also empower them by giving some loans to them in order to start a small scale business.

7.7 Organizing Seminars/Workshops

The church should be able to organize seminars and workshop for women at least once in a year. Sensitize women on certain issues such as marriage enrichment, Hepatitis, **HIV/AIDS** etc. and to teach women how to take care of a person living with **HIV? AIDS** in the church and even within the community. A specialist on a certain topics can be invited in order to give proper knowledge of the cause effects and the solution to some of these problems. Therefore, if the church takes these factors very serious as their part to play, women can be effective in the ministry of God.

7.8 Economic Empowerment

Economic empowerment women who are known to be bedrock of home are generally observed as the poorest in the society. Because most women are still in defiance of their husbands. Given opportunity to women are gate roots to insurance of eradication poverty ensuring total quality to family planning and reproductive health services. This no doubt will bring balance between population and availability resources and ensure sustainable patterns of consumption and means of producing.

The absent of economic privileges on the side of women has stopped them from becoming independently economically. The absence of such privileges have opens women to become venerable to unhealthy practices which brings diseases of different types such as **HIV/AIDS, STDS,** hard labour among many.

Another thing is that, all the time, women are the receiving end, and because of lack of economic empowerment, when something happened to their husband either trible accident or death, some cannot support themselves. Therefore some women involved in the habit of prostitution in order to take care of their children because they cannot feed them, and pay the school fees of there children during the absent of their husband and this can also made them to be affect with some disease too which will be a problem of her children also. Therefore is a call for the Church to stand in the gap to help women to be important and respect through economic empowerment.

CONCLUSION

From the trend of the studies, we saw women in scripture have demonstrated their God given potentials in fostering the work of God. In the light of this paper we could deduce that pastoral ministry is not limited to men, but women inclusive. God who made them male and female has his purpose to be fulfilled in the life of his creation.

As our studies have shown we have seen the empowerment of women in both the Old Testament and New Testament. And in a special reference in Acts 2:1ff we can see the Holy Spirit on both men and women empowering them for service.

But it is indeed very unfortunate to some of our Churches today who would not want sufficient participation of women in ministry. Therefore, women have the right to participate in every aspect of Christian life and service is statement that there is no Jew nor Greek, there male nor female for you are all one in Christ Jesus (Gal. 3:28) NIV. Such Pauline statement "let a woman learn in silence with all submissiveness and I permit no woman to teach or to have authority over men, she is to keep silent (1Tim.2:11-12) were directed against the heretical women that

Paul described in the context of the passage."[35] Women were viewed as imitators of Christ they endured the suffering of this life with patience in silence."[36]

Furthermore, our Churches need to encourage the empowerment of women to actively participation in the ministry. The truth is that the earlier the Church involves them, the better for all of us because if the unbelievers are using women in business to sell their products, why can't we learn something there and use them positively by allowing them to also be at fore front of the ministry. And the work of God will prosper in the ministry of the church.

BIBLIOGRAPHY

Bdilia, A. Bitrus et al, The progressive History of the Ekkesyar yan'uwa A Nigeria (EYN), (Jos: Midland press), 1998.

Bruce, Michael and Duffield G.E (ed.), Why not priesthood and the ministry of women, (Abindom: Marcham manor press), 1972.

Chilver, M. Alan (ed.), Women's ministry in the church: An African perspective, (Jos: Theological and Christian Education commission), 1997.

Clouse, Bonnidell 2 and Clouse G. Robber, Women Ministry, (Illinois: Intervarsity Press), 1989.

Cunnigham, Sarah (ed.), We Belong Together. Churches in solidarity with women, (New York: Friendship press), 1989.

Dali, Samuel Rebecca, Women in ministry with Jesus. Where are they? (Jos: Annet Production), 2000.

---

[35] Bonnidell Clouse and Robbert G. Clouse, Women Ministry, (Illinois:Intervarsity Press), 1987, 12.

[36] *Ibid.,* 13.

Evans, Mary, Women in Bible, (London: The Peternoster Press), 1983.

Hackman, R. Galen, "Sarah Right major. "Preacher" An introduction to Brethren History, (Mubi: published by TEE College), 1992.

Kouzes, James and Posner Bamy, The leadership challenges, (San Francisco: Jossey-Bass publishers), 1987

Nasimyu, Anne, "The church: Enabling and empowering of women in Africa," in Africa Christians studies, December 1995. Vol. 11.

Lockyer, Herbert (ed.), "Women" The illustrated Dictionary, (London: Hodder and Stoughton), 1987.

Macquarrie, John, The westerminister Dictionary of Christian Ethics, (Hesville: Westminster press), 1967.

Stein, Jess (ed.), The Random House Dictionary of the English language, (New York: Random House publisher)

Thoman E. Norman (ed.), Classic Texts in Mission and World Christianity, (New York:Orbis Books Publisher), 1995.

Tucker, A. Ruth. Women in the maze: Question and Answers on Biblical Equality, (Illinois: Intervarsity press), 1992.

Victor, O Musa et. al. Mission focus Mobilizing Christian for mission, Jos: Vol.1 No 2, May-August 2006.

Church and State:
Who Cares for the Poor?

Eta Eyolle Elvira

Africa is one of the most blessed continents in the world. Her blessings range from Cultural, economical, social, political and religious. She is the very continent that has suffered from colonial influences and has greatly robbed her of her blessings. African states like Liberia, Chad, Sudan, Mozambique, Angola, Ethiopia, South Africa, Zimbabwe, Cameroon and many others, due to political manoeuvre, have rather been a fertile ground for their colonial masters. The prevailing atmosphere has plunge this prestigious continent into financial crisis and the consequences are highly felt by the poor in African Communities.

Political bodies like the Organization of African Unity (O.A.U) sprang up but failed to deliver the goods. Its short sightedness to the major plights of Africans rather gave birth to dictatorial or authoritarian regimes. The spirit of apartheid resurfaced in other forms and as such, has rendered the continent at the mercy of the giant continents in the world. The political fight gave birth to the New Partnership for African Development (NEPAD) whose aim is to come up with economic policies that will help boast up economic cooperation and integration among African states. Due to lack of political and economic liberation NEPAD is defunctioned.

While political fights were going on, the Christian family saw a need of forming ecumenical movements like the WCC, WARC, and All African Conference of Churches (AACC) to address some of these issues. The latter movement over the years has been concerned with "the formation of Christian leadership informed with the reality of the continent". The AACC in order to accomplish this, has been organising programs and activities geared at equipping Christians and the young people to face the challenges of the continents. The church is seen as the main instrument to provide an answer to the ongoing financial crisis affecting the world and particularly the poor in Africa.

The Church

The term "church" is defined by the [1]Oxford Advanced Learner's Dictionary as "a particular group of Christians".[2] John H. Oak defines it as "the people who are called by God in Christ (I Cor 1:1, 2 and Eph. 2:19)" The word church can be "God's people called out of the world". The church is also seen as a community of brothers and sisters (faithful believers). It is according to this notion that Christ took upon himself the role of the builder of the Church (Mt. 16:18). Implying that, he is and remains the centre of the church. Jesus gave specific instructions to his disciples or followers about caring for the weak and needy (Pastoral care) in the community. These instructions specifically were geared towards the poor, as he came for the poor and not for the rich or righteous. In order words, he was breaking down the commandments to loving ones' neighbour as oneself. The church is seen as an arm which is directly concerned with the caring of the poor, the vulnerable, the voiceless and the downtrodden. Mtt. 25:34-40 says, the church has the responsibility to feed the hungry, give water to the thirsty, be receptive to the strangers, clothe the

---

[1] The Oxford Advanced Learner's Dictionary.

[2] John H. Oak, Healthy Christians make a Healthy Church.

naked, care for the sick and prisoners. The biblical instruction has no condition attached to it. The pastoral care insinuated is aimed at producing harmony (unity) amongst God's people.

Viewing the activities of the early church in Jerusalem, they strictly kept and put into practice Jesus' teaching. The Jerusalem church as described in the book of Acts serve as a model for the church of today as they strived for unity or togetherness. They took up the idea of benevolent gifts seriously. Acts 4:32ff describes the kind of life style which was lived. The gap between the rich and the poor was bridged as the act of sharing or community living was encouraged by the Apostles. The Apostles kept, to Jesus' teaching and Paul says "in everything I did, I showed you that by this kind of hard work, we must help the weak, remembering the words the Lord Jesus himself said; it is more blessed to give than to receive, "Giving/helping the needy is an imperative for the Christians Church. The church leaders were conscious of their responsibility towards the poor. The gospel was not only preached but was practiced. God's people need complete liberation from the hands of the oppressed and wicked.

Jesus the role model for the church did attend to the worries of the poor. He was hated by the Pharisees for being a friend to such persons. Jesus never discriminated upon the poor rather he showed them love, gave them hope and human dignity. The case of the lepers is instructive. The lesson put forward by Jesus Christ was for his followers to carry on the garment of love, peace, justice and transparency. The above mentioned qualities is highly to be practiced by the Church in the world and Africa today. The Church truly has the responsibility to bring not only spiritual renewal but complete rebirth in the continent of Africa. The Jerusalem church as earlier cited has its challenges and responsibilities which might not be very different from that of the African continent today, since "the Church in Africa is not a separate entity vis-à-vis the universal Church." The Church (churches) have the responsibility to put into practice sincerely Jesus' teaching. The role of a restorer must be taken up seriously by the Church in order to give the poor their rightful place in the society. Humanity was created in the image of God therefore all stand to be equal. There should be no room for discrimination or comparison amongst God's creation. The Christian Church in Africa over relied on the foreign religion. Worthy to mention is the fact that her rich culture and traditional religion has much to reckon with than learning on imported faith. The church stands to be the body of Christ and all her activities must be Christ centred; as he is the head of the Church. The Church is to "care for the flock that God has entrusted" to her (I Pt 5:2).[3]

THE STATE AND THE POOR

The word state can be defined as "the government of a country or a country considered as an organised political community controlled by on government". A state is governed by human beings. The government of a state is made up of people considered to be put there by God. Biblically, their authority comes from God as stipulated in Rom. 13:1-7. Also, in the bible we read about nations that were set up and the Lord raised up kings, judges and prophets including responsible leaders to run their internal affairs. The people of Israel were chosen and set aside as God's own. Bad leaders came up as well as good leaders, God allowed all these in order to glorify his name. The people or nation of Israel knew that without God they were finished. Paul recognises the fact that there is the need for people to have respect for government. This can be evident as they obey the rules and regulations put in place to maintain peace, and order. Paul draws this inspiration from Jesus' teaching wherein he said "give to Caesar what belongs to Caesar, and give to God what belongs to God" (Roms 20; 25). In

---

[3] André Karamaga, "The Challenge for Moral Regeneration in Africa" in Africa, step forth in Faith, edited by Nicholas Otieno, Kenya, 2008, p.151.

other words, Jesus was merely emphasizing the importance of submitting to human authorities and the God. He recognised the fact that God is the supreme authority, who in turn bestows it unto those who are chosen to lead the people. Apostle Peter in writing to the Christian Community, urged the leaders to care[4] for the flock God has entrusted in them. The state ruled by a government has the obligation to care for the poor, fight for their rights and dignity. The state must ensure that in her national legislations or in signing any international legislation, the needs and total wellbeing of the poor must be taken into consideration. Besides, the above the rich have often stood at the unproductive angle. Such an atmosphere led to oppression of the poor masses, marginalisation and exploitation. Coming to the African context, it is glaring that her states have greatly been exploited by the rich giant western countries. The poor in Africa are exploited culturally, politically, socially, economically, ethically even religiously. It's because of such dehumanised phenomenon that God had to step in with the act of liberation of his people (the poor) from the hands of the rich and the strong. He chose that the Messiah was to be born in a poor community , the one who really experienced and lived the life of the poor. He could best address their plights and worries out of experience. The state is to protect the poor in setting up structures to address their situation. The role the state plays is embarrassing to all, affecting justice, peace and human dignity at all levels. Speak for the voiceless, liberate the oppressed, and provide basic needs for the poor, (food, shelter, clothing, health and good drinkable water). The state can only do the above through her leaders from the top to the grassroots.

The reason why the Messiah came was to liberate humanity from bondage (enslavement of poverty, sin and all other vices). The setting of human beings free from whatever enslavery was a redemptive act understood from the biblical perspective. The

---

[4] The Oxford Advanced Learners' dictionary.

argument of complete liberation has often been projected and a clear conclusion not arise at since, states are governed by rules and laws which are either accepted by the people or imposed on them.

THE PREVAILING SITUATION

The poor in Africa and the world at large are to be given special attention. Coming to the African continent, she had been robbed of her riches by the colonial powers and subjected to wars, poverty, misery, hunger, bad governance and sickness among many other things. Till today, she is suffering from colonial manipulation but in more modified forms. She has lost the grip of so many things due to the current structures put in place. Such has led to suspicion, lack of confidence, and self-esteem in the lives of the poor in Africa.

The poor have often been thought to be useless, dependent and are more of a liability.

Coming to the reality of the matter, both the church and the state are in the struggle to care for the poor especially in the African context. The plights of the poor which ranges from discrimination, bribery and corruption, injustice, poverty, unequal distribution of resources, begging bad governance, marginalisation, globalisation and political and economic manoeuvres are being addressed on daily basis by either the Church (churches) or the state (states).

The coming together of denominations to form ecumenical movements both at international and national levels is to ensure that the poor are taken care of. Their plights are top priority for the church and as taught by Our Lord Jesus Christ, keen attentions for quick solutions are being taken. It is awful for one to note that, most of the decisions arrived at ecumenical meetings usually end as paper work. Practical realities are far fetched. The driving force behind such attitude is that most of the Churches have been structured in a way that many church leaders tend to safeguard or secure their positions and shy away from implementing the decisions. The church has rather been turned into a protective ground for the rich and strong. There is this common adage that "the church is hospital for sinners". Obviously, treatment is expected to be administered so as to free them. It is the reverse as many will hold that "the Church is an incubator for sin'. The church (es) aught to be the voice of the voiceless, a freedom ground. Today, the cankerworm of corruption, bribery, immorality, injustice, tribalism, discrimination has eaten hard in the church (es). Many term the churches to be a money making institution.

It is worthy to mention that the church has joint the other structures of the state in building hospitals, schools, training centers, communication departments and many other departments, to cater for the needs of the people and the poor in particular. Most often, the above mention institutions are used as a tool to generate huge sums of money for the church. The churches often say they are helping the poor. No doubt, the act of helping goes with discriminatory tendencies. Those in command will prefer desperate relatives, friends or neighbors to benefit than stretching out to those who actually need it. The church has become a fertile ground for embezzlers and they are only being changed from one department to another.

Jesus asked Peter; "tend my sheep". The same is being said to the church. One begins to wonder aloud where the church is heading to when their responsibility of tending has been turned to shattering. The idea of meritocracy is not the obtainable even in the church. Transparency and truth has greatly been turned down by those in authority. Some spiritual leaders have lost their spiritual grip and are turned to materialism. Today, the divine mandate to the church (es) to liberate the poor is gradually giving way, since, individualistic or egocentric tendencies are eating deep in to them.

The state is not left out. Many decisions and policies are being tabled but implementation is a problem. The issue of meritocracy is minimized in most sectors in the Cameroonian context. The chances of the poor are often given to the rich in competitive examinations due to the influence of money.

Jesus' teaching has not been given heed to. Many servants of God will prefer to attend to the rich than to the poor. In Cameroon, some of the Priests, Pastors, and those entrusted with the gift of preaching have been lured with money by the rich. Many at times the servants of God will prefer to devote all their time and energy were they will be rewarded heavily in financial terms. They have often despised the worries of the poor. We have church leaders who have often attended all the occasions that take place in cities or rural areas. Such leaders visit with a lot of expectations. Most church leaders are turned to secular living. Their standards do scare the poor to come closely, since they feel they have nothing substantial to offer. Spiritual leaders squeeze the poor and pay less attention towards their plight. This is evident as little or nothing so strong is being said by them in connection to the current atmosphere in the country. They have lost their prophetic voices and it is due to the fact that the same government officials are those found in church and they boost up the churches finances.

Thus, "robbing Peter to pay Paul". The corrupt nature of the church and the state has gone to enhance the ongoing financial crisis in Africa and the World.

PROPOSALS FOR A WAY FORWARD

After the above research and experiences, the following might be of help to the church and the state in relation to caring for the poor.

- These two institutions are to work in close collaboration in order that they can check on their implementation strategies towards the poor masses. Also the church has to re-instate her moral and spiritual authority in the organization of human matters.

- Identification of the plight of the poor is first of all important and the biblical solution of reaching out should be put into practice.

- Constant stock taking should be made with the poor involved at all levels, be it in Church or at the state level.

- God calls humanity to serve him in various sectors and in different ways. So, let each person examine his/her call and respond to it properly. The church's prophetic voice must be heard to the ends of the world.

- The need for communal living should be re-instituted at all levels.

- The Bible should be highly practiced or lived. Therefore, Africans should stop depending on the Westerners and depend on God, so as to squarely address and liberate themselves from the ongoing financial crisis and poverty. The church leaders should ensure that all the vices currently existing in the African continent (church and state) should desist. The Christian doctrines stipulated in the Bible should be practiced in the Church and the society will follow suit.

THE AFRICAN WOMAN AS A BREAD WINNER OF THE FAMILY

Africa being a patriarchal society, with the men as the pillars of everything from politics, to the economy, to Religion, the woman's place was considered to be in the kitchen. She had no voice in the running of affairs in the house or in the society. Despite her divine role given her by God as a helper (Gen 2:18), she was totally relegated to the background.

Now our days the men are gradually discovering the role of the woman (girl child). Today in Africa and in Cameroon in particular, many Families are led by women. Women's empowerment in all works of life is enabling them stand squarely to face the tasks of bread winning in most Families. Gradually some men are seeing them to be real helpers and others see them even beyond.

Coming to the Christian milieu, the woman is not different from the man. Many of our churches are full with women and they are so instrumental in the worship life of the church (es). Perhaps it due to this that the P.C.C (Presbyterian Church of Cameroon) might have thought it wise to incorporate the women into the Ministry of word and sacrament. Today, her spiritual background goes to project her even in the political sphere. In Africa and the world at large, one will scarcely hear of a woman embezzler. Their compassionate and loving nature stands to make them benefit the role of breadwinners in the community.

The woman today is known to have left the farm to the pulpit, the kitchen to the classroom, to the parliament and even up to the presidency. This new trend taken up by this humble creature in this millennium has actually changed the mentality of the Africans and most Cameroonians. The woman is most cherished and highly welcomed in the administrative arena. Thus, African and the Cameroonian woman get up and take your rightful place in the church, Family and in the society at large.

CONCLUSION

In this 21st millennium, the popular cry is that Africa is the continent which is most hit with poverty. The current situation is because the obtainable had been neglected by the institutions concerned. To Ngwa Julius Ambe, it "is not to say Africans are not responsible to certain extend..."[5] The care for the poor is a

---

[5] Ngwa Julius Ambe, "From political liberation to economic Liberation" in Africa. Edited by Nicholas Otieno, Kenya, 2008, p. 64.

divine obligation to both the church and the state. None of them is left out. All are involved to fight out the plights of the poor. Jesus fought right to the cross. His example must be emulated so that God alone can take the glory. Hence one can conclude that it is the duty of the church and the state to care for the poor.

Violence Against Women: A Challenge to the Churches in Northern Nigeria

Koni Patrick

INTRODUCTION

There is no doubt that violence against women is a painful reality seen and experienced by women daily, and at the same time it is an extremely sensitive issue for women. The contextual experience of violence against women in northern Nigeria, as well as those in other parts of the world, can contribute to a more differentiated picture. The fact is that the issue at stake has been and will continue to be a serious challenge in the church and in the society, unless something is done about. This is because it is not only limited to women but has repercussions on the relations of men and women, education of children, community building etc

The question here is how is violence against women manifested? How can it be stopped? What is the role of the church in Northern Nigeria on this issue of violence against women? These and other related questions will be the heart of this paper. "to take a close look at the aspect of violence. How can we deal with it, instead of just preaching to people to become nice and stop acting violently? How can we address the root causes of violence?"[1]

Violence against women is a problem that has to be seen on a phenomenological level as affecting all religions. For the purpose of limitation the present article will focus on the experience of Christian women. The research motivation is based on the observation that a number of women have suffered violence from the very people with whom they are closely related, Christian women have been obliged to hide or even deny the facts that violence exist in their homes due to the sense of shame and humiliation which they would probably have to go through if it became known.

To this end, however, the article will explore the topic in relation to the Contextual description of evidences of violence against women and the theological implication for the churches in Northern Nigeria.

However, the researcher would like to emphasize the fact that, this issue is a reality for women and at the same time a taboo subject which needs to be addressed openly, especially by the religious leaders, in order to help stop violence against women.

Finally, this article is also intended as a contribution towards the end of the Decade to Overcome Violence (DOV), launched by the central committee of the World Council of Churches at its meeting in Berlin in February 2001, and which will be concluded by the International Ecumenical Peace Convocation in Kingston/ Jamaica in 2011.

---

[1] Ucko, Hans, Ariane Hentsch(eds.), *Changing the present, Dreaming the future: A critical moment in interrelations   dialogue.* (Geneva: WCC publications), 2006   p. 25.

What is Violence?

The word violence according to Alleluia and Johnson "is problematic. This is because every definition is influenced by the cultural values that shape the way particular groups of people choose to live in any given society."[2] The idea here is that what is deemed as violence in one society may be viewed as acceptable behavior in another society. While acknowledging the relevance of this assumption, however, the researcher will use the definition of violence given by the World Health Organization. The WHO (World Health Organization) defines violence as. "The intentional use of physical force or power, threatened or actual, against oneself, another person, or against a group or community, that either results in or has a high likelihood of resulting in injury, death, psychological harm, maldevelopment, or deprivation."

Based on my findings, I was able to discover that there is no generally accepted definition of violence against women. Some writers would prefer a broad definition such as structural violence which includes poverty, health and education. For others, it refers to structural social mechanisms by which a woman is forced into a subordinate position. Those who advocate the earlier concept use it in order not to lose the actual description of power as being the force behind violence against women. To me, both definitions offer valid aspects to the analysis of the phenomenon which can be examined in turn.

> "any act of gender-based violence that results in, or is likely to result in, physical, sexual or psychological harm or suffering to women, including threats of such acts, coercion or arbitrary deprivation of liberty, whether occurring in public or in private life."[3]

---

[2] Alleluia, Filemoni-Tofaeono and Johnson, Lydia, *Reweaving the Relational Mat: A Christian Response to violence against women from the Oceania,* (London:Equinox publications), 2006, 1.

[3] *http://www.un.org/rights/dpi1772e.htm* Retrieved on May 3, 2010.

Based on the above mentioned definition, one could say that violence is directly connected to the use of power. Power according to Mayland is "physical strength, political, or institutional. It has the overtones of aggression and authority." Power is often used on women at home, in religious places and in the community at large, therefore one can conclude that power becomes abusive when the desire to exercise control is attached to it. But "All of the interwoven strands of violence...trace their origins to a patriarchal construction of power".[4] The patriarchal use of power as stated above without any doubt is the origin of violence against women. However, it will be inappropriate to deny the incidents of violence perpetrated by women against men and against other women, but the fact remains that in the majority of cases violence is exerted against women.

Violence against women manifests itself usually in one of the following forms and frameworks:

- Domestic violence
- Physical violence
- Psychological violence
- Social violence
- Cultural violence
- Economic violence
- Educational violence
- Health violence.
- Sexual violence

All these are forms of violence that usually have an affect on women, but for the sake of conciseness, this paper will lay emphasis on a few of them which are directly tied to the contextual experience of violence against women in Northern Nigeria. These

---

[4] *Ibid.*, 8.

include domestic, physical, psychological, social and cultural violence.

ROOT CAUSES OF VIOLENCE AGAINST WOMEN

Based on my findings, I discovered that, it is difficult to relate accurate statistical data with root causes of violence against women, but a lot of elements were discovered to have contributed to or perpetuated violence on women. The patriarchal ideological practice in Northern Nigeria could serve as the major contributing factor to all from of violence on women. The patriarchal structure leads to subordination, discrimination, and control behavior which legitimized women in the society. However, the following factors could be seen as some of the root causes of violence on women

- Patriarchal ideology and the misinterpretation of religious beliefs

- Women's low status and powerlessness

- Dependence on men as a result of poverty

- Gender-biased parenting: boys right from childhood are being trained to see girls as inferior which may lead to abuse on women in their adulthood

- Lack of forgiveness and genuine love, dignity and respect for human rights

These and many other elements foster the spread of violence against women in Northern Nigeria

General Overview of Violence Against Women in Northern Nigeria

In this section, I would like to talk about the link between religion and culture in connection with the patriarchal use of power, as two of the most used tools of violence against women, after which the ethical implication of the problem which involves the violation of human rights will be considered, as well as the value and the dignity of human as being created in the image of God

The issue of gender inequalities, although a global phenomenon with deep historical roots, resonates particularly with the Nigerian context. Chenyere affirms that,

> *"Gender relation in Nigeria is characterized by a lot of imbalance to the disadvantage of women. This is the twenty first century yet tradition, culture, religion, and other factors have continued to widen the disparity between a man and a woman by keeping women in a subordinate position to men .The larger society and the male sub-culture still see women and their aspirations as subordinate resulting in a situation in which the marginalization, trivialization and stereotyping of women are glaring aspects of Nigeria today".[5]*

Most people in Nigeria do not recognize and accept the reality of violence against women. The point here is that, as long as it remains a secret issue, it is most likely to be considered as non-existent, irrelevant or not an issue at all. Religion in my understanding, should be viewed as an area where gender barriers should not be promoted especially in Christianity. Aruna Gnanadason rightly commented that the "church's statements condemning violence against women are still few and far between, or are incorporated into other statements so that the specificity of women's experience of abuse does not get the attention it deserves".[6]

It is also interesting to observe, that in religious instruction offered by church institutions in the country mainly personal morality is emphasized, whilst the social aspect is often neglected. The message is always for women to be submissive and for men

---

[5] *http//:www.portal communications.com:gender and communications in Nigeria, is this* the 21st century Dr. Stella Okuuna, dept of mass communications A.N.U Nigeria 2002. Retrived on the 8/12/2008 (no page number).

[6] Gnanadason, Aruna; *No longer a secret: The church and violence against women.* (Geneva: WCC publication),1997, 40.

to love their wives. While this makes reference to the biblical injunction, which needs to be respected, the church needs to go deeper into the meaning of such words emphasizing the uniqueness of an individual and the will of God in marriage.

For example the Apostle Paul in (Eph 5:25) says that "Husbands love your wives as Christ loved the Church and gave himself up for her" to reflect on this statement, a question could be asked, how many Christian husbands today demonstrate such love to their wives? On the other hand, in (Eph 5:25) women were asked to submit to their husbands as to the Lord, this biblical injection together with the influence of the culture of subjugation of women has a lot of impact on Christian women. In their majority women guide their way of life in connection to that injunction. However, few women as mentioned earlier, turn out to be the perpetrators of violence themselves, majority of women act in such a way as to defend and protect themselves from men's authoritative and oppressive role vis-à-vis women. This offers another fruitful field of reflection on how gender relations could be constructed differently in flowing from a commonly experienced and recognized relationship with Christ.

Cultural Impact of Violence in Northern Nigeria

Whenever we talk of culture, we are referring to the way of life of a particular group of people which includes their beliefs, customs, practices and social behavior.

"There needs to be recognition that the African context is diverse and that each context has its own specific challenges. Hence it is important to identify and describe oppressive cultural and religious practices in each context".[7]

---

[7] Chitando, Ezra and Hadebe Nontando: *Compassionate circle: African women theologians facing HIV,* (Geneva:WCC publications), 2009, 10.

In the context of Northern Nigeria, the culture and the religion of the people has been influenced by the Islam doctrine, "Section 55 of the Penal Code Law from the Laws of Northern Nigeria (1963) states that: 'Nothing is an offence which does not amount to grievous hurt upon any person and which is done by ... a husband for the purpose of correcting his wife'"[8]

This is part of Shari' a law which is based on the Islamic teaching. Even though this law is not binding for Christians, who are free to practice what their religious principles teach, however, the practice has impregnated the mentality of large parts of the population in Northern Nigeria, and has even become common among Christians.

The truth remains that culture has both positive and negative effect on the people. As Christians, there is a need to understand that absolute goodness can only be found in gospel, the goodness of culture comes in only if it those not violated or contradicts the scriptures, the gospel should transform our culture not the other way round.

In connection to that I will like to emphasize the fact that culture in the northern part of Nigeria is a major contributing factor that fosters the spread of violence against women. Within the framework of this culture the care about the ill-treatment of women is not promoted. Adequate support for abused women is

---

[8] *Http/:www.leadsnigeria.org.* LeadsNigeria –creative awareness among Nigerian women. 16 days global campaign to highlight gender violence. Retrieved on the 26/4/2010.

This is an organization known as "league of Democratic women" concerned with the free and legal rights violation of women and children under the Directorship of Rebecca John Sako. Henceforth a reference to the above document will be used as "Leads Nigeria–creative awareness among Nigerian women. Highlight on gender violence."

not provided, mainly because by gender equity and equality encouraged.

The use of the word equity in the sense should be seen in terms of a good and fair treatment of all humans with respect and dignity. More to that, culturally in most African societies, the belief is that, culture has given men the right to be violent which is accepted as a norm of the society. It had already put a wide gap between men and women this wrong notion has made so many women feel isolated and intimidated so that the fear of inferiority complex is always around them, they hardly speak in the midst of men because of fear or shame. Female students in schools, bible study classes, and in some Christian programmes or public places will prefer to keep quite, to them, it is normal for a woman being silence in amidst of men.

The predominant cultural pattern of silent submission greatly influenced women's behaviors such as to bear violence as the legitimate use of patriarchal authority.

> "...for most Nigerian women, the culture and religion of the land has turned them into powerless humans beings, the culture supports this practice by making it socially acceptable to batter a woman and by expecting her to silently endure any ill-fate that befalls her in her matrimonial home."[9]

In some ethnic groups, the widows are considered people of no value especially if childless, in some traditions the relation of a deceased man will have to offer the widow to a husband, otherwise everything, including the children will be taken away from her. Women who are yet to have a child are being humiliated by both men and women in the society. Decision making in this cultural

---

[9] *"Leads Nigeria–creative awareness among Nigerian women. Highlight on gender violence."*

context is usually made by men, without the consent of the woman, a women's son can be called instead of her for a discussion which relates to the family in the absence of the husband. Women are being harassed by their in-laws which in most cases lead to divorce. High bride prices also could be considered as a major contributing factor, as a result of which women are being treated as salves not with dignity and respect. However, the manifestation of violence could be seen in the following forms.

Domestic and Physical Violence

Violence in the northern part of Nigeria occurs in almost all the forms of violence mentioned above. "Domestic violence is often not seen as a social problem but as a private matter between a man and his wife. In many cases it is accepted as a part of 'married life' and as a normal means of discipline of a woman by her partner"[10] this could be a reflection of the situation of some women in Northern Nigeria, who enter into the matrimonial home with the idea that they may be beaten by their husbands at any time when ever they make a mistake. For some women this constitutes a perpetuated experience of female oppression as their mothers also had to bear this violence. This intergenerational transmission has lead to such a strong normative plausibility that an external interference, even by neighbours and close relatives, would be interpreted as intruding into private affairs. The privatization of violence against women makes people, even the religious leaders, being afraid of publicly advocating against violence on women. Oduyeye comments that, "Wife beating is one aspect of domestic violence around which a heavy cloak of silence is drawn".[11]

---

[10] *Created in the image of God: from hierarchy to partnership. A church Manual for Gender Awareness and leadership development,* (Geneva: WARC Publications), 2003, 122.

[11] Oduyoye, Mercy Amba. *Daughters of Anowa: African woman and Patriarchy.* (Maryknoll, N.Y.: Orbis Books), 1995, 166.

By way of emphasis, this beating happens not just inside marriage, but also outside, it occurs in boy/girl friend relationships, in courtship, among youth and students of all academic levels, and irrespective of age. Domestic violence also occurs in areas where burdens and work load are being put on women/girls. For example, working on the farm and doing all the house-work which includes cooking, sweeping, fetching water, in some cases from a far distance, dish washing, bathing the children, washing cloths, getting firewood for cooking is mandatory for women, domestic violence may not be so rampant in the urban centers as a result of technological advancement, but it also has its own form which may be different form those in the villages, but it is a reality in the rural areas.

Another form of domestic/physical violence manifest in the areas such as, slapping, punching, kicking, threatening with weapons such as knives, woods, stones, and sexual violence such as forced pregnancies is also common, men transmitting STDs, especially HIV/AIDS, to their wives, men going away from home in search of better economic conditions, sometimes leading to abandoning their families back in the villages without sending any remittances.

Time and again one can hear men describing their wives as "machines for producing children", reflected sometimes in the inhumane habit of urban migrants to visit their families once or thrice in a year with the sole intention to impregnate them. Infidelity is also common. Some men keep girl friends or concubines which increase the tensions in a household, augment the volatility and facilitate the exertion of violence against women.

The misconception associated with violence in the Northern part of Nigeria manifests itself as follows

- Domestic violence is a private affair between a husband and a wife

- All domestic work, regardless of the condition of the woman, is her sole task

- Violence does not occur in the community because the culture allows a man to beat his wife as a corrective measure or as a sign of love.

- Some women deserve to be beaten as a corrective measure

- Domestic violence only happens to poor uneducated women and women who live in the villages

- Only drunks and never-do-well people beat their wives because of poverty

- Domestic violence is non-existent because of modern living-conditions

In connection to misconception that women who are educated does not experience violence because of the status, a story was told about a couple who are both educated, the wife is never free to do things her own way, she is always being controlled by the husband, the husband always lives a vibrant social life while the woman is always indoors. She has all the comfort money can give, yet her life resolves around the house. She has no social life. She cannot move an inch without the consent of the husband; if she does then beating will follow, she has never compliant, she admitted that the culture allowed men to discipline his wife and of course she has to stay for the sake of her children and her marriage

> *"Many battered women have either lost their lives or have been maimed for life. A man in Bauchi State, Northern Nigeria, cut off his wife's right leg, in a fit of jealousy for allowing a male doctor to administer injection on her. A woman in Kaduna state, Northwest Nigeria suffered a miscarriage as a result of severe beatings from*

---

[12] Leads Nigeria–creative awareness among Nigerian women. Highlight on gender violence. (no page number)

her husband who accused her of having extra-marital affairs. The stories are endless and the statistics are rising...... Family pressure, societal attitudes, lack of economic power, obedience to religious injunctions, coupled with the attitude of law enforcement agents who trivialize issues of wife battery, are some of the reasons why most battered women stay on".[12]

The above-mentioned misconceptions, which are associated with the traditional beliefs, could be considered as some of the basic elements that promote violence against women in the community. Also, the majority of women are lacking knowledge of what constitutes abuse. The truth of the matter is that, it is a general and widespread problem which can happen to any one irrespective of class, social status in the community, religion or age.

"Studies have shown that a man who regularly beats his wife or partner and children may be a perfect gentile man outside the home. He may be a Doctor, minister, lawyer, psychologist, teacher or other profession who will never be violent to other men or women in the public sphere. He can control himself out side, but pick a safe target inside the home".[13]

So many women have lost their lives through violence and rarely are the perpetrators declared guilty.

Psychological Violence

Psychological violence happens often such as verbal abuse from the husband, refusing to provide adequate money for the housekeeping, especially women who are totally dependent on their husbands for their livelihood, criticism, public humiliation, intimidation, threats, derogatory remarks supported by the influence of parents and friends. An anecdotal report on a newly married couple may illustrate this:

---

[13] Gnanadason, Aruna; *No longer a secret: The church and violence against women.* 8.

> "Ami, the newly married bride, walked into the sitting room carrying a heavy tray filled with goodies destined to be ravished by her husband's friends. She served them all and took a seat next to her husband. The men there were engrossed in a Controversial debate about Nigerian politics, Ami; confident about her intellectual abilities to contribute constructively offered her opinion. At the sound of her voice the noisy room fell into silence. The men thought an interruption like this by a woman was abominable. How dare her! They looked at her suddenly filled with disgust and completely failed to appreciate her contribution. Ami's husband grabbed her badly and dragged her out of the room. He screamed at her incoherently saying she should never interrupt their conversation. After all, their religion and culture did not permit a woman to talk when men were talking. The yelling and beating was the beginning of their problems in marriage."[14]

My interpretation would be that violence or threat of violence against women arises when they dare to attempt to interfere with the established cultural power of men. Men often use derogatory remarks and say all kinds of abusive words about their wives. They would rather consult their families or friends on issues relating to their families than discuss it with their own wife. A man would rather prefer his wife to be a spectator in the home than a participant in the decision-making process on family matters

Economic Violence

This form of violence is also very common. However, the disparity of situation has to be noted as well as the fact that economic violence does not manifest itself in a uniformed manner. Most

---

[14] Posted by: Misi cukar on Nov, 29 2007 Africanloft: *News, commentary and social media from African perspective*: *http:// www.africanloft.com/african-culture-and-religion-fuel-cruelty-to-women/.* Retrieved on 28th April 29, 2010.

women in the rural areas suffer from the economic violence. They have to work hard in order to provide food for the family. They go to the farm every day in the rainy season or engage in different kinds of business which sometimes leads to harassment and humiliation, in some instances, the product of the farm harvest will be sold by the husband with or without the consent of the woman and instead of being appreciated for her hard work, mortification follows. In all of this, the women would have to remain loyal and submissive to their husbands; their only intention is to not to break their marriage and also to cater for their family. Some men do not have time to spend with their family, how the children are being brought up in good moral way is not their concern. Their main role is serving as discipline masters in their own homes.

Ethical Implications

Human rights are the fundamental right of each and every one to enjoy certain basic needs which are considered as constitutive of human existence, and include the ability to survive, freedom of expression, association, and equality before the law. The Universal Declaration on Human Right, according to the United Nations stated that, "All human beings are born free and equal in dignity and rights. They are endowed with reason and conscience and should act towards one another in a spirit of brotherhood."[15] These are the rights that are considered by most societies as belonging to everyone, e.g. the rights to freedom, justice, and equality. The Bible also is not silent on the issue of human justice. Therefore, the injustice, lack of freedom, respect, and dignity, of which women in the northern part of Nigeria are being deprived should be given full consideration. The spiritual life of a Christian should be the reflection of his/her daily living. Hence, fundamental respect for each human being which includes

---

[15] *http://www.un.org/en/documents/udhr/*. *Universal Declaration of Human Right*. 1948 Retrieved on April 27, 2010.

a commitment to the rights and dignity of women should be an ethical concern of every Christian. Even though some of this violence takes place in the secret, the point is that, nothing is hidden from God. Remember all have will have to give account of his/her deeds before God.

THEOLOGICAL REFLECTION: THE ROLE OF THE CHURCH IN RESPONSE TO VIOLENCE AGAINST WOMEN

Experiences and observations has proved that the church has not been effective in addressing the issue of violence against women for decades, the silence over such moral issues in Aruna's idea, was a genuine and proved fact by WCC (World Council of Churches) In her visit to more than 300 member churches to reflect on the issue of violence against women, the findings shows that, majority of the churches are aware that violence against women is real, while other denied that, violence against women happens only in the neighborhood.[16]

The denial of violence against women is common specifically among men who claim to have been given the Authority and the power by God to have all the power and to use it as he wants. Nevertheless, the reality of violence as experienced by women in Africa today is a great challenge to the churches in Northern Nigeria; women in Africa are the back bone of the church. They have been involved in social work, ministry and evangelism just to mention but few. The Church has been concerned about their involvement within the church setting, but, less has been said about their difficult moment outside the church.

The church which serves as the reflection of the Christian community and as agents of transformation by bringing the kingdom of God on earth, there is a needs to be holistic in its

---

[16] Gnanadason, Aruna, *No longer a secret: The church and violence against women.* 72.

approach in the sense that, social justice with regard to the violent act being committed on women daily should be part of the message of the church. Knitter affirms that, " the kingdom is a life style characterized by justice, peace, and goodness in both personal relations and social and economic structures. Hence, when religions promote the oppression of women in whatever way, they are to be judged as being against the kingdom"[17] Even though, it is a well known fact that, "The history of the church has been one of reinforcing the patriarchal values in the society."[18]

A lot of secular organizations in the world today have recognized the evils of violence against women as the highest form of violence in the society.

The church, as well as any other religious institution, has a great role to play in influencing the social, ethical, moral and the spiritual life of its members. Christian women are looking up to the church to serve as their savior in this difficult moment. The scripture is very clear in its approach to violence against all creatures.

Theologically, the abuse or the destruction of God's image is a sin before God; both men and women are created in the likeness of God. (Gen 1:26) Sin is a state of bondage that rules over and distorts human life; it is turning away from God's will for humanity which leads to sinful acts such as that of exercising power over, or controlling and abusing women. The act of domination as practiced by the perpetrator of this act is usually supported by making reference to (Gen 3: 16) which says *"your*

---

[17] D' Costa, Gavin; *Christian Theology and other Religions: An Evaluation of John Kick and Paul Knitter In: Studia missionalia*: Theology of Religions; Roma, publication of the faculty of Missiology, Gregorian University, vol. 42, 1993.

[18] Gnanadason, Aruna. Et al., (Eds). *Women, Violence and Nonviolence Change.* (Geneva: WCC Publications), 1996. 60.

desire shall be for your husband and he shall rule over you". This text could be interpreted as the result of sin entering the world and is a clear description of fallen humanity for which Jesus has suffered to redeem humanity. Usually the message has been that, women and children are the property of men as people with power of control. Bohn has argued that, the description of man's claiming to have the ownership of women has been preserved as the normal accepted social behavior of the society, therefore, the use of violence on women is normal way of extending ones right of ownership.[19]

In this situation, what should be the response of the church? The Statement of the Faith and Order Commission of the WCC in its book entitled *'The Church and the World'* stated that, "in Christian tradition men and women are created in the image of God, who has been revealed as the communion of love of the Father, of the Son and of the Holy Spirit. Men and women as the image of the triune God are, therefore, intrinsically relational. **They become fully human as they live a life that reflects the relations that exist among the Trinity"** (Bold passage by the author).[20] We are all one in Christ Jesus. The apostle Paul in (Gal 3:28) declared that there should be no discrimination among men and women. Jesus Christ, specifically in the pattern of his lordship, humbled himself and became a servant, he did not call his disciples servants but friends. A question could be asked, how many husbands call their wives as friends with whom they can share ideas? The Holy Scriptures also made it clear that men and women are equal partners who should share in solidarity with one another.

---

[19] Bohn,Carol; *Dominion to Rule: the roots and Consequences of a theology of ownership; In: Christianity, Patriarchy, and Abuse. A feminist critique;* Carlson Joanne Brown and Bohn R Carol (Eds). (Cleveland: pilgrim press publications), 1989, 106.

[20] Faith and Order commission: *The Church and the World: The Unity of the Renewal of Human Community,* (Geneva: WCC publications), 1992, 57.

Therefore, to remain silent over this issue should not be considered as an option for the Church. If the churches are to proclaim justice to all humanity, violence of any kind must be a sensitive issue which the church needs to preach against. To be silent over such an issue makes the church lose its credibility on moral issues and with regard to its pronouncements on the dignity of all humanity.

One of the fundamental problems that exist in the churches today is one of discrimination, women are the majority but their impact is not felt. The church should take it as a point of duty to involve women in discussions, decision making, and leadership positions to recognize and to appreciate their presence in the church, the church has the responsibility to teach both men and women the biblical precept of living together, for women to respect their husbands and for the husbands to respect their wives too. Denouncing all forms of violence and encourage men to recognize the rights of women as created in the image of God.

CONCLUSION

In conclusion I would like to say that all human behavior is learned and it can be unlearned. Therefore violence against women can be unlearned as well. The solution to this problem has to start right in the homes. The male children need to be educated on how to respect female for a cohesive and productive society. The relationship between a man and a woman when built on mutuality, respect, sharing and love can be very meaningful for both as Christians, Jesus identified with women and people who suffered violence; a typical example could be the case of the woman who was caught in adultery. (John 8: 11) The unjust penalty that was pronounced on her was lifted by our Lord.

It is an imperative that clergy, church leaders and the entire church community learn about the secret form of violence that is happening in our churches in Nigeria today. Religious leaders can utilize their position as community leaders to shape the life of their members within the context of religious teaching, The use of such verses which are used by the perpetrators in subjugation of women need clear and practical interpretation, for example in (Gen 3: 16) which says *"your desire shall be for your husband and he shall rule over you"*. This text could be interpreted as the result of sin entering the world and is a clear description of fallen humanity from which Jesus has suffered to redeemed humanity. In any case the word 'rule' does not mean acts of violence. Often, the struggle against violence on women is viewed as women's problem which dose not concern men, it is apparent that women are often the victims of higher forms of violence in our community be it visible or invisible, but the only solution to the problem has to come from men and the church at large.

The Faith and Order Commission of the WCC advocated that "the role of the church is to restore and to liberate the suffering image of God."[21] The church should identify with those vulnerable women to value and respect the image of God that is in them. It is important for the clergy to take this issue seriously.

Lastly, a serious issue which the church needs to pay much attention to is the issue of culture. The church needs to stand firm in areas where culture seems to overrule the biblical injunctions, especially by supporting violence against humanity and God's creatures at large. The church should redefine its position from the biblical perspective especially on the areas of ethical issues, human relations, family affection, freedom and the liberation of all creation. May God grant us the Grace to live peacefully with one another irrespective of our gender for the world to see the light and the Glory of the image of God in us.

---

[21] Faith and Order commission, *The Church and the World: The Unity of the Renewal of Human Community*, (Geneva,:WCC publications), 1992. 57.

BIBLIOGRAPHY

Allleluia, Joan Filemoni-Tofaeono and Johnson, Lydia; *Reweaving the Relational Mat: A Christian Response to violence against women from the Oceania,* (London:Equinox publications), 2006.

A Faith and order study Document, Nr. 151 Church *and the World, The Unity of the Renewal of Human Community,* (Geneva: WCC publications), 1999.

Bohn,Carol, *Dominion to Rule: the roots and Consequences of a theology of ownership* In: *Christianity, Patriarchy, and Abuse .A feminist critique;*

Carlson Joanne Brown and Bohn R. Carol (ed). (Cleveland: Pilgrim press publications), 1989.

Bond Janet-Nash (ed), *Churches say no to Violence against Women.* (Geneva: The Lutheran World Federations), 2002.

Chitando, Ezra and Hadebe Nontando, *Compassionate Circle: African Women Theologians Facing Hiv,* (Geneva: WCC publications), 2009.

World Alliance of Reformed Churches(ed.), *Created in the image of God: from hierarchy to partnership. A church Manual for Gender Awareness and leadership development,* (Geneva: WARC Publications), 2003.

D' Costa, Gavin, *Christian Theology and other Religions: An Evaluation of John Kick and Paul Knitter,* In: *Studia missionalia:* Theology of Religions; Roma, publication of the faculty of Missiology, Gregorian University, vol. 42, 1993.

Eastern and central African Women in development network, *Violence against Women: A trainer's manual,* (Nairobi : Pauline's Publication), 1997.

Gnanadason, Aruna, *No longer a secret: The church and violence against women,* (Geneva: WCC publications), 1997.

Gnanadason, Aruna (ed), Women, Violence and nonviolence Change, (Geneva: WCC Publications), 1996.

Mayland, Jean, *Breaking the chains of the past of the Church teaching on Violence against Women; Theological reflection and suggestions for discussion and action,* (Lower Marsh: Churches together in Britain and Ireland), 2003.

Nason, Naney Clark, *The battered wife,* (Lious: Westminster John Knox), 1999.

Raiser Konrad (ed.), *The Ecumenical Review.,* Vol. 54, Nr 3, July 2002. Together with Courage. *Women and Men living without Violence against Women,* (Geneva: WCC Publications), 1998.

Ucko, Hans (ed), *Changing the present, Dreaming the future: A critical moment in interrelations dialogue,* (Geneva: WCC publications), 2006.

Oduyoye, Mercy Amba. *Daughters of Anowa: African woman and Patriarchy,* (Maryknoll: Orbis Books), 1995.

World council of churches(ed), *Streams of Grace,* (Geneva: WCC Publications), 2005.

INTERNET SOURCES

www.who.int/violenceprevention/approach/definition/en/index.html. Retrieved on the April 26, 2010

Dr. Stella Okuuna, dept of mass communications A.N.U Nigeria 2002. www.portalcomunicacion.com/bcn2002/n_eng/ programme:gender and communications in Nigeria, is this the 21st century. Retrieved on the 8/12/2008

Leads Nigeria –creative awareness among Nigerian women.16 days global campaign to highlight gender violence (copyright 2010) Retrieved on the 26/4/2010

http://www.leadsnigeri.orgindex.php?option=com_content& task=view&id=14&Itemid=29

Posted by: Misi cukar on Nov, 29 2007 Africanloft: News, commentary and social media from African perspective: Retrieved on 28th April 29, 2010 *http://www.africanloft.com/african-culture-and-religion-fuel-cruelty-to-women/*

http://www.un.org/en/documents/udhr/. Universal Declaration of Human Right. 1948 Retrieved on April 27, 2010.

"The Hem of His Garment": Perspectives on Christian Cure and Healing in Cameroon

Perpetua B.N. Fonki

INTRODUCTION

"Suffering, misfortune, disease and accident are all 'caused' mystically"[1]…as far as most Cameroonian people are concerned. Christianity has attempted to demystify and dissolve these concepts, but is still to satisfactorily fill the vacuum it has created, by shifting these deeply internalized concepts away from customarily held beliefs to Christian beliefs. The Christian missionaries to Cameroon (Jamaican born Rev. Joseph Jackson Fuller; 1825–1908, a Baptist missionary, and later by Jamaican born Joseph Merrick and the Englishman Alfred Saker) at the onset of the gospel were very committed to the belief they were propagating. After the early death of Joseph Merrick, Rev. Fuller became very instrumental in the spread of the gospel. He was well noted for his humorous and eloquent preaching, which caused the local chiefs and in Bimbia in the south west region of Cameroon to give up their old ways and pledge to follow what he had in store for them. The work of Rev. Fuller and subsequent

---

[1] J S Mbiti, *African Religions and Philosophy.*

missionaries tainted indigenous Cameroonian practices and beliefs as invalid, malicious or inferior. The result was a vacuity that had to be filled by an unconscious importation of the traditional beliefs into Christianity, or acculturation which is a very recent Christian move.

Prior to the arrival of missionaries, cure and healing were the monopoly of diviners and medicine men. Unfortunately these were the people who were chastised most by the missionaries at the onset of Christianity and still are today. Most of their methods were and are still crude and can not be explained scientifically thereby rendering a substantial part of their practice unacceptable. Their links to the spiritual were and are still defined as witchcraft and black magic by their Christian counterparts. Some of these practices were only recognized as a form of religion very recently. The general name given to this has been '*African Traditional Religions*' since each tribe or group has unique practices. The 'notorious' religiosity that the Africans practice as purported by Mbiti[2] is more rooted in their traditional religions, than it is in Christianity. The traditional religion and Christianity are in a constant battle among the Cameroonian Christians, each yielding at different instances. The result of this is that anything in Christianity that is a little close to the traditional religion sells high.

The diviners for instance are held very high in esteem by the community because they believe in a life being remote-controlled from the spirit world. The only person that has the powers to influence what button is pushed on the remote controller is the diviner or medicine man. For the Christian, this role is taken over by the clergy. The clergy is regarded as one who has the power to intercede on their behalf, and also convey messages from God. In the search for answers to their problems and appropriate

---

[2] *Ibid.*

diagnoses for their diseases, most of the Christians have entrusted their lives in the hands of their clergy. This upright trust has instilled confidence in some ministers, facilitating their ministry in an incredible way; while others have been unnecessarily pumped up by it to the extent that they have become miniature gods to their people.

Before Christianity was born, the crowds that followed Jesus Christ in search of signs and wonders outnumbered those who come to seek for salvation. Churches and denominations that preach and actively focus on the healing and cure ministry, have a population explosion, while those who have maintained the traditional missionary dogmas and liturgical trends have either dwindled, or maintained a struggling growth. The reason is simple. Just as Jesus Christ had to constantly deal with crowds each suffering from different forms of ailments, so does the contemporary Christian church in Cameroon.

The reasons may be very different from those of the people that followed Jesus Christ, but the trend is similar. This has led to a reframe of liturgies and a tilt of theological ideologies to fit the needs of the yearning people.

John S. Mbiti posits that in "African villages, disease and misfortune are religious experiences, and it requires a religious approach to deal with them".[3] The surging rate of unemployment and poverty is not blamed on the government alone. Sometimes unemployed and unsuccessful people blame their predicament on supernatural forces, usually within or without the family. Unemployment causes poverty, which leads to the mishandling certain minor ailments that could be tackled easily with little resources. Unfortunately, these minor diseases become chronic with time, and force the sick to use unconventional methods in search of a cure.

---

[3] *Ibid.*, p.169.

There is however, a shift from the traditional medicine practitioner or diviner, to Christianity. This trend is not a virgin pattern of behavior as far as the search for wholeness is concerned in Cameroon. There is a constant paradigm shift from the local healing medium represented by the 'native doctors' and sorcerers to the church. The church seems to be doing a great job in convincing people that the saving power of Jesus Christ is more than that of traditional medium. Neil Cosslett in his book *The Healing hands* emphasizes the notion that Jesus Christ was in constant opposition to sickness.[4] Each time he encountered a situation which involved sickness and diseases; he used authority to eradicate it. (p. 66)

The contemporary Cameroonian society is plagued with a lot of circumstantial chaos that creates a very conducive atmosphere for either emotional or physical ailments. The root cause of these could either be due to political, economical, psychological, or sociological reasons. This has culminated in the ardent need for some form of wholeness, either through holistic healing, or through cure. I like to make the difference between healing and cure. In this paper, cure is the restoration of physical health while healing incorporates both physical and emotional.

This catalyzes several questions: Why has there been a sudden increase in this trend? What is lacking in the mid century liturgies adopted by the mainline Christian churches in contemporary Cameroon? Why has there been an increasing shift from the communal problem solvers- the medicine man or the sorcerer to the church? Why does the Mass Media record an increase in audience on radios and channels that project TV Evangelists that focus on healing and cure? Is the deviation from preaching to healing or cure, for the people who come or for the self aggrandizement of the perpetrator? Has Christianity done enough

---

[4] Cosslett, Neil *His Healing Hands.*

to build trust in life after death, the way African traditional religions have? This paper explores and tickles some of the issues prevalent in Cameroon and its environs.

Christian Healing in Cameroon

Most mainline denominations in Cameroon are relaxing their grip on traditional liturgies introduced by western missionaries. This has led to a type of dynamism in congregations to the extent that it is difficult to find two congregations of the same denomination in Cameroon, with a uniform style of worship. Most doctrinal issues are left untainted, but most preachers have revised worship services to take a therapeutic focus. Preachers have coined their messages more to appeal to the pews, while giving them some kind of hope and reassurance. It is common for people to endorse the preacher who coins his preaching to what I call "feel-good" messages. Some mainline denominations' worship styles are increasingly being modified by Pentecostal and charismatic influences. These Pentecostal or charismatic churches are not African indigenous churches, yet their approach to Christianity has become increasingly attractive.

Some congregations in the Presbyterian Church in Cameroon have designated special services for healing, while others have incorporated varied forms of healing services in the Sunday worship. There is also a group of others who believe that all they do in ministry contributes to the holistic healing of the individual, and they think that the emphasis placed on healing by some is exaggerated. The subject of healing in Cameroon needs careful attention, by both the perpetrators and the skeptics.

The Presbyterian Church in Cameroon (PCC) belongs to the association of the protestant Churches in Cameroon with the acronym CEPCA. This is the group of churches that is metamorphosing the most in the onset of the trend. The Presbyterian Church in Cameroon has a book of orders which has which guides both the pastor and the Christians in worship. There is also "The Book of Divine Services"; a liturgical set used for worship, each volume emphasizing different aspects of worship. On healing, volume four of the PCC *Book of Divine Services* section II which is 'the ministry to the sick and to the dying' stipulates the structure of the service. The structure of the ministry to the sick has the salutation, the introduction, the act of penitence, the ministry of the word, the ministry of intercession, the laying on of hands, and Holy Communion. This liturgy has been modified by pastors who have incorporated healing services in their congregations to include anointing, and blessing of holy water and crosses. Exorcism has also been incorporated in these services.

Homiletics has also been revised by many clergy involved in these 'healing services'. It is common for preaching during such services to be responsive and punctuated by outbursts and cries. Africans are a very expressive people. This expression is very spontaneous and sometimes formal liturgies are very inhibiting. Emotional outbursts are a vital component of the Cameroonian culture. When the local king who is considered the mediator between the people and the spirit world appears, he is greeted with boisterous shouts and shrills. When he says something appealing to the people he is cheered up. The preacher in the church is seen in this role. Hence any form of worship that introduces the familiar, gains total acceptance.

This sway owes its existence to Pentecostalism. Pentecostal churches are Western born, yet mainline denominations modifying western liturgies replace the voids with Africanized Western Pentecostalism. Allan Anderson in writing about the fortes of Pentecostalism posits:

> "Many forms of African Pentecostalism have liberated Christianity from the foreignness of European cultural forms. A sympathetic approach to African life and culture, fears and uncertainties, and an engagement with the

African world of invisible forces, have been major attractions of these churches to people oriented to a world of both evil and good spirits. This is accentuated in the South African Black townships today, where rapid urbanization and industrialization have thrown people into a strange, impersonal, and insecure world where they are left groping for a sense of belonging. Pentecostal churches, with their firm commitment to a cohesive community and their offer of full participation to all, provide substantially for this universal human need in a positive response to the problems of modernity. They give solutions to basic human problems, especially healing from sickness and deliverance from a seemingly malevolent and capricious invisible world. Above all, they offer a baptism of power that enables a person to overcome the threatening world of unpredictable ancestors, spiteful sorcerers and inherently dangerous witchcraft. The spirituality of Pentecostalism was in fact a new and holistic approach to Christianity that appealed to the African imagination more than older forms of Protestant Christianity had done."[5]

The onset of this trend the PCC was plagued with chaos and confusion. There was modification of worship styles in some congregations and the term used was 'revival'. A lot of dust was raised by this concept. This was either because the approach was that of a drastic change or because the form of worship in the church had been internalized to an extent that any modification was considered a betrayal. This led to a revision of the "Book of Orders" of the church to include a section on "Revival in the Church".

In section 11.3 and 11.4, it states that:

"In principle, the PCC encourages revival in the Church: because a church which ceases to revive, fails to grow.

---

[5] Allan Anderson,Pentecostals and Apartheid in South Africa during Ninety Years 1908-1998 University of Birmingham.

> Thus the PCC appeals to all its Christians to follow the revival guidelines approved by synod in 1994 for Christian growth and maturity. Revival should be a means by which God, through the Holy Spirit edifies and unifies His church, which is the body of Christ. Unfortunately, there is a certain spiritual trend in the PCC now, in the name of "Revival" which, in the view of the Synod Committee inhibits unity and Christian growth instead of promoting them."[6]

This is just one of the processes of transformation involved in spicing a reformed liturgy with a Pentecostal touch. The reframe is not a monopoly of the protestant churches. The Catholic Church adopted acculturation during the last two decades and it boosted their membership in many parishes. They have a long tradition of healing or cure in Cameroon. Effigies of the Virgin Mary, the rosary, holy water and the anointing oil are used by the Christians to replace the traditional amulets that were condemned at the onset of Christianity in that region. The healing liturgy however, is being influenced by the charismatic movement in the Catholic Church. This new interest to healing is not unique to Cameroon or Africa, but has a global appeal. Those that are a little slow in joining the van wagon due to authentic fears are faced with the problems of losing their folk to others or losing trust.

Recently I read an article *Witchcraft destroying the Catholic Church in Africa* from the Catholic Information Service for Africa. In it, Scholars from the Catholic University of Eastern Africa (CUEA) posited that the dismissal of the issue of witchcraft in the Catholic Church as mere superstition has disastrous consequences. "Because they do not get adequate help from pastoral agents, they seek the assistance of witchdoctors or join the mushrooming evangelical denominations that offer healing, exorcism and

---

[6] PCC Book of Orders.

deliverance, they said."[7] This goes to confirm the popular adage that a drowning person can grab even the tail of a snake, mistaking it for a rescue rope. Whoever offers what seems to be first aid, thrives and gains the trust; be it the traditional diviner or the clergy.

Michael Katola, a lecturer in Pastoral Theology at CUEA states:

> "From the African perspective Christianity does not seem to have answers to all questions. And while the church demonized traditional experts such as medicine-men and diviners, it has offered no equivalent alternatives, he added. We have many Christians who go to consult fortune-tellers when they want to start a project or when faced with problems, he said. Africans are not any more superstitious than other peoples ... The problem is that the church has not come to terms with the African worldview which accepts the existence of evil powers, he said. It is important for the church to understand the fears of the people and not to attribute them to superstition. Witchcraft is a reality; it is not superstition...many communities in Kenya know those powers exist in their midst. Dissatisfied Catholics are swelling the ranks of the new evangelical movements, he said. Many of our Christians seek deliverance, healing and exorcism from other denominations because priests do not realize they have redemptive powers...the responsibility of fighting witchcraft lies with the clergy, who should start by accepting the reality of the phenomenon. If we don't believe in the existence of witchcraft as Satanism then we can not deal with it."[8]

The Catholic Church in Cameroon is taking this seriously and the constant growth of charismatic movements within the parishes is proof of the importance given to the subject. It has not yet received total acclamation from the conservatives or the skeptics

---

[7] Katola, (2007).

[8] *Ibid.*

and they have legitimate reasons to resist. Does this popularity of Pentecostal influences mean 'a square peg in a square hole' to fill the void in the Cameroonian Christian? Just as in the African traditional environs, people run the risk of falling into the hands of counterfeit 'native doctors' or diviners, so does the Christian church in Cameroon.

Snags in Christian Healing

An African proverb states that 'smooth seas do not make skilful sailors'. The yearn for cure and healing in our churches in Cameroon are issues of great concern. It does not suffice to dismiss the attitude of some who want to satisfy the Christians by mirroring whatever they lay their hands on. It is a challenge that calls for the church dogmaticians to think out of the box, reframe inflexible worship lifestyles, while externalizing straight-jacketed colonial Christianity from the conservatives and replacing with Africanized Christianity. The delayed response or lack of it has led to some congregations adapting secular trends and branding them as religious. It is very common now our days to see a lot of hip hop culture in the congregations, adapted from the western media. This has even influenced the instruments that are used in praise during worship. Bands are becoming very popular in the congregations. Less attention is given to the local musical instruments which are readily available. It is very easy to mistake the praise time in some congregations for a street festival. I think this reduces the awesomeness of worship and erodes the culture of the people. The target is to enable the people have a spiritual 'high' which is a vital catalyst in healing services, so what ever it takes is good enough.

Healing services are accompanied by a lot of kickbacks, so some clergy have made maximum use of this resource to the detriment of the church and the Christians. This has brought about a lot of deceit, lack of trust, and betrayal. Neil Coslett emphasizes that "the Pastor is the conscience of the people- the only trusted and truthful individual".[9] Eagerness to be accepted as powerful healers has led some pastors into falsehood and deceit, thus producing a ricochet effect.

Rev. Samuel Kabue, a Kenyan Presbyterian minister addressing delegates at the World Council of Churches' Conference on World Mission and Evangelism on the theme "Come Holy Spirit, Heal and Reconcile", warned that religious groups that proffer "miraculous healing" and traditional denominations that stress a "charity approach" are alienating disabled people from churches. He further stated that People with physical challenges feel alienated, marginalized, embarrassed and in some cases offended by the way they are treated in some churches. Some churches "have made the word healing an anathema in the ears of persons with disabilities". He warned against "commercial fixes and religious groups which offer miraculous healing in the setting of superficial acceptance and friendship".[10] Such violation is very common in healing services. Most often those who do not have positive results are branded as having weak faith, or hiding something that they have not confessed. They face a chastisement not just from their Christian environs, but also in their neighborhoods.

The Hem of his garment: Revisiting Jesus Christ's Healing Ministry

The woman in the gospels who had been bleeding none stop for twelve years, must have tried all she could to make herself clean. The fact that she lived during the Jewish era when a woman undergoing menstruation was a '*niddah*' [considered unclean] until all the required cleansing rites and duration separating the period

---

[9] His Healing Hands– Neil Cosslett.

[10] Stephen Brown,Churches Urged to Respect the Disabled in 'Healing' and 'Charity' Ministries, *May 11, 2005 http://gbgm-umc.org/ global_news/full_article.cfm?articleid=3201.*

from blood free life were observed. No one wants to remain in an unclean state for some hours, let alone twelve years. She would do anything to have her normal life restored to her. She heard about Jesus, and probably saw the miracles he performed; restoring wholeness back to people.

> "When she heard about Jesus, she came up behind him in the crowd and touched his cloak, because she thought, "If I just touch his clothes, I will be healed."" Mark 5:27-28 (Today's New International Version)

> Wherever He entered, into villages, cities, or the country, they laid the sick in the marketplaces, and begged Him that they might just touch the hem of His garment. And as many as touched Him were made well. Mark 6:56

Unfortunately, many have used the idea of faith and trust in Christian healing to be biased and judgmental on those who have not seen any changes in themselves after healing services. Some have pretended to be cured, and shielded their pains from friends or neighbors because they are scared to be thought of as faithless. This attitude contributes to the deceit and the wrongful portrayal of 'quacks' in Christian healing and cure. Some of this 'little or no faith concept' comes to chastise the sick and exonerate the clergy. Jesus Christ never refused to heal anyone who asked for his help. He may have traced the root cause of some illnesses to families and curses, but he never sent people home the same way the came under the excuse of a lack of faith. His actions sold his personality.

> "And when the men of that place recognized Jesus, they sent word to all the surrounding country. People brought all their sick to him and begged him to let the sick just touch the edge of his cloak, and all who touched him were healed." Matthew 14:35-38 (Today's New International Version)

Jesus faced some instances where people refused to believe him and showed complete faithlessness and distrust.

> Is this not the carpenter, the Son of Mary, and brother of James, Joses, Judas, and Simon? And are not His sisters here with us?" So they were offended at Him. But Jesus said to them, "A prophet is not without honor except in his own country, among his own relatives, and in his own house." Now He could do no mighty work there, except that He laid His hands on a few sick people and healed them. And He marveled because of their unbelief. Then He went about the villages in a circuit, teaching. Mark 6:3-6 9 (New King James Version)

Yet he laid his hands on a few sick people and healed them.

The Christian basis for healing lies both in the great commission and in the epistles.

> And He said to them, "Go into the entire world and preach the gospel to every creature. He who believes and is baptized will be saved; but he who does not believe will be condemned. And these signs will follow those who believe: In My name they will cast out demons; they will speak with new tongues; they will take up serpents; and if they drink anything deadly, it will by no means hurt them; they will lay hands on the sick, and they will recover." Mark 16:15-20

This is the core of the Christian mission. Are Christians in Cameroon sticking to this or has this mission been derailed? This calls for further discussions.

> And God has appointed these in the church: first apostles, second prophets, third teachers, after that miracles, then gifts of healings, helps, administrations, varieties of tongues. Are all apostles? Are all prophets? Are all teachers? Are all workers of miracles? Do all have gifts of healings? Do all speak with tongues? Do all interpret? But earnestly desire the best gifts. And yet I show you a more excellent way.

Healing is for us. 1 Corinthians 12:28-31

Jesus Christ prayed and laid hands on people for healing. That is the theological basis for the omission of anointing in; *The Book of Divine Services,* volume four of the Ministry to the Sick' of the Presbyterian Church in Cameroon. The Concept of anointing the sick is only found in the epistles.

> [14]Is any one of you sick? He should call the elders of the church to pray over him and anoint him with oil in the name of the Lord. [15]And the prayer offered in faith will make the sick person well; the Lord will raise him up. If he has sinned, he will be forgiven. James 5:14-15 (New International Version)

Jesus Christ commissioned us his followers to his ministry. We strive to be good imitators of Christ. However, some of the chaos that goes on in the name of healing in Cameroon and neighboring countries raises a lot of questions in my mind. I know God transcends all human limitations, including chaos and acts for our good regardless of our intentions. "Nobody likes to see spoiled or demanding children throwing tantrums in a toyshop or being rude, nasty, and thoughtless because the required sweets are not forthcoming. How sad it is to see a child who is always 'on the want' treating parents just as necessary providers instead of responding to them in real love. And yet, how easy is it for us to slip into this kind of pattern in our prayer-relationship with God, to be always wanting, often thoughtless, and even abusive when we don't get our way"[11]

I attended a healing service once and witnessed a lot of physical violence going on in the name of healing. The acceptable mood of healing is when the sick falls on the ground and goes into 'spiritual fits' while others scream on the top of their voices. The elders or deacons already anticipate these 'falls' in some denominations, so they stand behind the sick ready to catch or pull them down. In the case I witnessed, the young woman missed

---

[11] Cosslett, Neil *His Healing Hands.*

hurting her skull at the sharp edge of the sanctuary by millimeters. Then of course the explanation given was that there was a spiritual warfare between the demons and the Holy Spirit, and the demons were defeated, even though she missed cracking her skull on the hard surface.

In another instance, a young man refused to fall down in submission to the power the clergy had invoked. He was being pushed down by both pastor and intercessors, and he resisted, since he was very strong. He left from there cursing everyone in the church and calling the pastor fake. Another young man who was mentally challenged was taken to the church, because it is believed that he was possessed by evil spirits. The pastor had a very long whip which they used the beat this young man. It is believed that they were beating the demon out of him. This violation kept going on until another pastor who was sitting in the pews observing, stopped them by taking the young man away from them. Everyone cautioned him that this young man was possessed by the evil spirit and was going to become violent, yet he was so compliant to his rescuer.

Recently, a young man was brought to me at about 11.00pm. He had been showing signs of incoherency in the university, and his room mates took him to a Pentecostal church for prayers. He beat up the pastor and ran out. The room mates called his mother and she came to school to collect him. When she realized that her son was incoherent, she called a pastor she trusted very much so that he could be healed. Unfortunately, this pastor was in another town and asked her to see her home pastor. Her home pastor was not around, and she brought the young man to me. In my preliminary questioning, I realized that his mental aptitude was irregular. He was talking ills about some family members, and immediately, accusing fingers were being pointed towards these people. Then I asked if he could pray for us, which he accepted. I requested his permission to allow us hold his hands during prayers. The touch of his hands made me realize that he was running a very high temperature. I advised the mother after to take him immediately to the hospital. This young man was suffering from cerebral malaria. I do not know what would have happened if they kept praying for him without medical attention. I do not know what would have happened to the relationship between them and the accused family members, had he died.

CONCLUSION

An interesting number of Christians use both the 'native doctors' and the clergy for healing. It is difficult for them to trust the Christian healing completely, despite the fact that Christianity has propagated the power of the Holy Spirit over all other powers. These people still want to be sure and they do not want to loose either way. The blazing wave of healing and cure in the Christian churches in Cameroon owes its success partly to the belief that all sickness and misfortunes come from God. This is either punishment for some recalcitrant behavior of the sick or from the clan. The church then becomes the place where this can be reversed.

David Garland says in the NIV Application Commentary, "One need not look far to see preachers who do not preach to reach the people but preach to reach the top, to become ecclesiastical superstars. They see discipleship to Jesus in terms of rank and privilege. They assume that Jesus is someone who will achieve things for them and give them the status of the lords."[12] Some however are forced to assume this position because they want to belong. Christians validate preachers who have something out of the ordinary to flaunt. Those who are just ordinary hard workers with nothing extraordinary in the congregation are labeled unproductive or faithless. This has led

---

[12] Garland, (1996).

to hard work in some areas, or manipulation in others. The discussion continues: how do you tell the genuine ones from the fake ones; how do you authenticate the healing and cure that purportedly takes place in the congregations? Christianity is void of scientific proofs and relies on faith and belief. This only reiterates our human limitedness in attempting an in-depth understanding of the sacred through eyes of the secular.

And so I want to tickle us to further discussion from three quotes that I got from some of my most admired writers and from another religion (Buddhism).

> Mark Twain states; "In religion and politics people's beliefs and convictions are in almost every case gotten at second-hand, and without examination, from authorities who have not themselves examined the questions at issue but have taken them at second-hand from other non-examiners, whose opinions about them were not worth a brass farthing. - *Autobiography, 1959*

> Bertrand Russell writes; "What a man believes upon grossly insufficient evidence is an index into his desires — desires of which he himself is often unconscious. If a man is offered a fact which goes against his instincts, he will scrutinize it closely, and unless the evidence is overwhelming, he will refuse to believe it. If, on the other hand, he is offered something which affords a reason for acting in accordance to his instincts, he will accept it even on the slightest evidence. The origin of myths is explained in this way."

> In the writings of Buddha, "believe nothing just because a so-called wise person said it. Believe nothing just because a belief is generally held. Believe nothing just because it is said in ancient books. Believe nothing just because it is said to be of divine origin. Believe nothing just because someone else believes it. Believe only what you yourself test and judge to be true".

Remember, as humans, we see the outside; God alone knows the internal and all intensions.

REFERENCES

Anderson, Allan. (2000). Pentecostals and Apartheid in South Africa during ninety years 1908-1998. *Cyber Journal for Pentecostal Charismatic Research*, Cambridge

Brown, Stephen. (2005). Churches urged to respect the disabled in 'healing' and 'charity' ministries. *UMC Global News*, Retrieved from http://gbgm-umc.org doi: 3201

Cosslett, Neil. (1985). *His Healing Hands*. Channel Islands: Guernsey Press Ltd.

Garland, David. (1996). Mark. (1996). *NIV Application Commentary*. Texas: Zondervan

Katola, Michael. (2007). Witchcraft destroying the Catholic Church in Africa. *Catholic Information Service for Africa*, Retrieved from www.cisanewsafrica.orgdoi: 22994

Mbiti, S. John. (1969). *African religions and philosophy*. London: Morrison & Gibb Ltd.

Presbyterian Church in Cameroon. (1998). *Constitution*. Victoria: Presbook Press

Presbyterian, Church in Cameroon.(1991). *Book of Orders, Procedures and Practice of the Church*. Victoria: Presbook Press

Reconciliation and Transformation in the Feminist Perspective: Taking the First Step and Non Violence

Azange Margaret

1. INTRODUCTION

Anger, hatred, vengeance, non acceptance of guilt and bitterness seems a reality of our society and the world at large today. In our society, differences increasingly cause tension between people, groups and nations People are divided in many ways, including race, culture, gender, social class and religion. Human beings usually hold on how evil others are and always pointing accusing fingers at others while forgetting those fingers that point at self. The Lord Jesus Christ admonishes us to remove the long from our eyes then can we see clearly the speck in another person's eye. (Matthew. 7:3) We are going to write this paper, drawing our inspiration from Matthew 18:15-20 and 25-35 and Numbers 27: 1-11 where the offenders take the first step to reconciliation and transformation. Jesus Christ stressed, honesty, justice, diligence, active caring for others and reconciliation. God showed his love to the human race by initiating reconciliation with us while we were yet sinners by sending his only begotten son to die on the cross to cleanse us from our unrighteousness. Reconciliation is very important and this is why Jesus had to give up his life so as to transform the world. If he had waited for human beings to initiate reconciliation it might never had been. In these passages, we see qualities that should characterise the relationships of God fearing people. There should be peaceful reconciliation and when one party feels on the right and aggresses, it leads to further aggression. We must have experienced and known that "two wrongs do not make a right".

2. DEFINITION OF TERMS

To reconcile according to the Cambridge International Dictionary of English is "to find a way in which two situations opposed to each other are in agreement or become friendly again". Mennonite peace builder, John Paul Lederach, describes reconciliation as "a meeting ground where trust and mercy have met and where justice and peace have kissed". Reconciliation takes place with oneself, others and God. Differences and diversity nevertheless, does not call for reconciliation because they are normal happenings in any given society, due to the fact that people come from different culture and backgrounds. Their opinions could be different but all constructive, good and fruitful. Reconciliation only comes in when there is a wrong domination of opinion to exploit a difference.

Reconciliation, if need be, is therefore a process that requires a chain reaction in the following stages:

1) The parties or at least one of them should see the necessity for justice and peace. There should therefore be a commitment to justice and peace.

2) There should be a third party who identifies the matter at stake, thus a middle, non-partisan person.

3) The middle person discusses the matter individually with the bitter parties, where every bit of truth is unveiled.

4) The parties in bitterness are brought together, to face the facts revealed individually.

5) The guilty party or parties (both of them may have wronged each other in one way or another) may pledge guilty.

6) There comes confession of wrong done to each other.

7) The obstacle of bitterness is then removed between the parties concerned.

8) They both forgive each other.

9) The parties cast away all desire for retaliation and nurse positive feelings about each other.

10) Lastly, there is restoration of a broken relationship.

Reconciliation is very important and this is why the Roman Catholic Church considers it, as one of the seven sacraments they have and believe in. It therefore takes to reconcile, awareness, repentance, grace, repairing of damage, letting go, leaving all vengeance and rebuilding of a new and peaceful life together. When people reconcile, there comes a transformation of thinking, behaviour and attitude both spiritually and physically. This is because when people are in bitterness with one another, they nurse wicked and negative feelings about each other. When reconciliation takes place, the opponents become positive in their thinking and instead of avoiding each other or not being in talking terms, they start visiting and talking with a smile to each other.

This is a true Christian attitude because we stand in church and promise to follow Christ, saying, "Yes I will God being my helper". When a Christian is born again, changes in the person's life are gradual but sure. To change habit as an individual is very difficult but the Holy Spirit inspires Christians and there is an unconscious change that people see and marvel at the work of the Almighty God.

Transformation like reconciliation is also a process. To transform according to the Advance Learner's Dictionary, 6th edition, is a "complete change of appearance or character so that it is better" Transformation leads to positive change in form, shape, appearance, behaviour and life-style. These changes could take place in animals, things, individual human beings or the society as a whole. Better still, a leading author and researcher, George Otis Jr. defines transformation as "a condition of dramatic socio-political renewal that results from God's people, entering into corporate vision, corporate repentance and corporate prayer. During these extraordinary seasons, the Kingdom of God pervades every institution of human endeavour".

In a Conflict Research Consortium, University of Colorado, USA, 1998, we understand that:

> The term "conflict transformation" has been coming into increasing use in the past two decades. Prior to that, the most commonly used terms were "conflict management" and "conflict resolution." The difference signalled in the term "conflict transformation" is both in how we see conflict and how we move through it. Rather than a problem that needs to be fixed, conflict and the way through it are seen through multiple lenses that focus upon the participants in the conflict rather than solely on the issue itself. In order to do this, more than skills are needed.

Transformation needs faith, commitment, apology and forgiveness (Desmond Tutu said, "No future without forgiveness"). For true healing to take place, there are also stages:

1) Confession, where in the people involve, state the truth, acknowledging all the unjust and hurtful actions done against each other.

2) Repentance, where the parties turn from unholy actions to loving actions.

3) Reconciliation, where they express and receive forgiveness. After this, there is intimate fellowship with previous enemies.

4)   Lastly, there is restitution, where the people attempt to restore all the damages caused in the course of bitterness. Justice is then sought wherever possible.

When transformation takes place in human beings, especially in their life-style, there is an inner renewal and reshaping of mind. II Cor. 5: 17 reads "Therefore, if any one is in Christ he is a new creation; the old has gone, the new has come" (this is the greeting of the Christian Women Fellowship of the Presbyterian Church in Cameroon) This greeting is because when a woman becomes a member of the fellowship, the members and the society is expecting positive changes in the woman's life and prove her being born again in the Holy Spirit.

The change in character is not solely an individual effort but needs divine intervention. The person needing transformation has to sincerely repent, be humble and pray without ceasing. This will then attract the favour of God who will cause a break throw beyond human understanding. Let us use the example of the story of the prostitute in Lk. 7: 1-9, 36-50, who became conscious of her sins and went to Jesus weeping and washing Jesus' feet with her tears. She was not only conscious of her sins but was ready to repent of them and so she took all the risk, came to the home of Simon the leper to seek the Lord's favour. She was well known in the society negatively but as the song writer, Norman Macleod wrote, she ceased from man and looked above her, trusting in God and doing the right thing.

Transformation is a continuous process as long as we are on earth. People should learn everyday, leading to changes in activities and life-style. Transformation will only be complete and perfected when Christ returns and reigns on earth. At that time, "the will of God will be done on earth as it is in heaven", as we say in the Lord's Prayer.

The greatest sin is to be conscious of no sin, but a sense of need will open the door to the forgiveness of God because God is love, with arms open to receive any repentant sinner. Only those who realise the depth of their sins can appreciate God's forgiveness. When forgiveness takes place, the person wronged should try to forget whatever wrong had been done. The Lord says, "I will not remember their sins and evil deeds any longer" (Heb. 10:17).

Our Lord Jesus said on the cross, "Father, forgive them for they know not what they are doing". Despite the pains he was feeling, he still found a place in his heart to forgive the sins of those who trespassed against him. We could easily say or draw the conclusion that he did this as God and it will be difficult for a human being to have such a forgiving mind but it is not impossible.

Joseph, totally human is a model of genuine forgiveness. He at, about an age of seventeen, the brothers hated him for no fault of his; decided to get over with him. They sold him to the slave traders who took him to Egypt and back home they lied to their old father that an animal killed him. Despite the rejection from his brothers, the fact that he was kidnapped, enslaved and imprisoned, God showed Joseph his grace and he forgave his brothers and shared his prosperity with them.

God in his grace, showers sinful human beings with goodness even though they sin against him. Forgiveness is therefore a mark of Christian living, following the example of Christ. If people have experienced God's undeserved favour, then they will want to pass it on to another person, God being their helper because humanly speaking, it is a very difficult thing to do.

As a parish pastor since1993, we have experienced that forgiveness is very difficult and when people say they have forgiven each other, it is difficult to forget and bring in true restoration. As we grew up like children, we heard our parents and people saying "we are going to the mission to pass confession". Whenever we passed in the church compound, we saw a long line of people queuing up for confession. These days, we no longer see the line of people waiting to see their spiritual leader for confession. As a parish pastor, we interviewed some Christians and they said "the world is all evil and even the pastor is not free from sin so they cannot confess to them. To some, the pastors no longer know the importance of secrets. As you confess to the pastor, the next sermon is on the subject of confess and this is not to encourage but to make the person know that he or she is condemned. Some also accuse the pastor for being so occupied in other things (what the term tent ministry) that they do not have time to listen and advise the Christians.

People prefer the slogans, "Every person for himself, God for we all or, I do not feed from my opponent's pocket and only death will bring us together" These slogans should not come out of a Christians mouth because we are new creature in the Lord Jesus who died to reconcile us with God so we should follow his perfect example. Never the less, I always tell people when they say women like to keep a record of wrongs done by their husbands that it is human. When a wrong is done even though there is forgiveness, the scar remains and when that wrong is repeated, it hurts more because it touches on the scar. When restoration therefore takes place, the relationship becomes stronger when the offender tries to prevent repetition of the wrong or more mistakes.

We also experienced that Christians will not even want to bring their problems to the pastor for possible reconciliation and restoration. They will prefer just to avoid each other and remain enemies in one congregation or either change congregation or denomination. Every Sunday we call on the Christians to confess their sins so that they can be forgiven and we also ask them "to forgive each other as the Lord has forgiven them". In the Lord's Prayer we say, "Forgive us our trespasses as we forgive those who trespass against us".

The volume four of the book of Divine Services of the Presbyterian Church in Cameroon is for the Ministry of

Reconciliation. This volume is used for general confession before Holy Communion Services so that the people can confess their sins and also forgive each other. During the Communion service, the people are called to true confession. They are told; "if you bring your gift to the altar and realise that someone has something against you, leave your gift in the altar, go first and be reconciled". Despite all these, the ministry of reconciliation has been very difficult.

In the Roman Catholic Church, it is different because to them, reconciliation is a sacrament to prove its importance in what they believe and doctrine. They as Africans, ask the sinner to suffer the consequences of the sin by doing some manual work for a number of days depending on the gravity of the crime committed. Nevertheless, the number of people who come for confession is greatly reduced compared to what it used to be, because of the reasons mentioned before.

As Christians, even if an offender will not say sorry, forgive because this act will break a cycle of revenge, free one from a heavy load of bitterness and lead to mutual reconciliation. "If someone sins against you, spare not the effort to make that person admit the fault and to make things right again with you". This means that we should tolerate any situation in which there is a breach of personal relationship between us and another person. Such a discipline is always to be given in humble love and not in self-righteous condemnation but in a true desire for reconciliation.

Our Lord, in his mercy and grace, reconciled to the human race while they were yet sinners by sending Jesus Christ to carry the burden of human sin and thus reconciled us to God. What we are now expected to do, reconciling with one anther is just a consequence of divine action. The sinless Christ is identified with human sinfulness so that sinful human beings may be identified with God's righteousness. The message of reconciliation has been entrusted in the hands of the church. Let us remember," To air is human and to forgive is divine". Reconciliation is a healing ministry for both the offender and the offended. It serves to restore our graced relationships of love, harmony and friendship with God and neighbour.

Pope Benedict XVI's first encyclical, *Deus caritas est*, reminds us that our God is a God of love, a God who is Truth itself, and also rich in forgiveness, forbearance and mercy. Should not people who are committed to such a God lead the way through this polarization—not simply to avoid it or paper it over with some irenic bandage, but engage the parties at loggerheads with each other? Rather than leading the way to a deeper entrenchment, should not we as Christians find a way to a truthful and just rapprochement?

3.   EXPLANATION OF PASSAGES CHOOSEN

From the Old Testament (O.T.), we see the five daughters of Zelophehad, a father of the clan within the tribe of Manasseh who went to Moses asking for their rights. They were very courageous to speak so boldly at an official gathering of Israelite leaders. It was not reasonable for them to make such a request in the context of the ancient east where all social pressures were against women inheriting property. Experience especially in the African context proves that women have limited access to peace negotiation processes. The women despite their population majority, they have little or no representation in the government and all important decision making bodies. This limits them from voicing their concerns, interest and pains to the public. Women have suffered over labour, forceful and early marriages sexual abuse, forced into polyandry and social stigmatisation and marginalisation as the case of the daughters of Zelophehad. They nevertheless "faced the bull by the horn".

Their case was presented to the highest court which consisted of Moses as king, the princes and the congregation of elders. The young ladies made their application to the powers that be. They did not look for lawyers to defend them but managed their own cause wisely enough because it was plain and honest.

They petitioned that they may have a possession in the land of Canaan among the father's relatives. Numb. 27:4. God had said to Moses in Numb. 26:53 that he had faithfully made known to the people that the land of Canaan was to be divided among those that were now numbered. These daughters of Zelophehad knew that they were not among the numbered and therefore by that rule must not expect any inheritance. The family of their father has therefore to be looked at as extinct and written childless though with many daughters. They gave a hard thought to this and prayed to be admitted heirs to their fathers and also to have an inheritance in his right.

They pleaded that their father died under no attainder which might be thought to have corrupted his blood and confiscated his estate but that he died in his own sins, Num. 27:3. He was not involved in any rebellion against Moses but in normal human and for which he will stand judgement like any other human being. He was never convicted by anything that might be a barrier to the children's claim.

It was a difficult case for Moses to take a decision especially as it concerned the society. To be on the safe side, he took the case to God, the righteous judge who will not look at the human mind to take a decision. He judged the case in favour of the daughters of Zelophehad and for all future occasions. On this occasion, a general law was given that "in case a man had no son and dies, his estate should go to the daughters Num. 27:8. Not to the oldest as the eldest son but to all of them in co-partnership Num. 27:9-11. If a man has no issue at all, his estate shall go to his brethren, if not to his father's brethren and if still none, then to the next kinsman. These children, consulted not only for their comfort and credit of their family but for the honour and happiness of their sex.

Let us now go to the New Testament (N.T.) passage. Matthew: 15-18 and 21-35, This passage does not sound a reality from a human point of view. William Barclay in his commentary thinks that this passage is not a correct report of Jesus' words because:

1) Jesus could not have made reference to the church because it did not exist while he was on earth. The church was only formed after Jesus had ascended into heaven and sent the Holy Spirit on Pentecost day to empower the disciples, who then came out to preach the word of God.

2) The passage speaks of tax collectors and Gentiles as irreclaimable outsiders. We know that one of the accusations against Jesus was that he was a friend to tax collectors and sinners.

3) Jesus never spoke of tax collectors and sinners as hopeless but with love and sympathy. "I have not come to call respectable people but outcasts" Matt. 9:13b. Matt. 21:31b also reads to conform this, "I tell you: the tax collectors and prostitutes are going to the Kingdom of God ahead or you", talking to the teachers of the law and the Jews who saw themselves having a privileged position in Heaven.

4) The passage does not ends with the accession there is no limit to forgiveness. The evil one should never be abandoned as beyond hope and condemned for hell, as long as the one lives, covered by God's grace.

Nevertheless, our concern for this passage is the fact that we should spare no effort to forgive sin and the first step is to be taken by the offended.

Matt. 18:15-18 makes us understand that a Christian community is to be ruled by love and forgiveness and not by a series of rules and regulations. As Christian, we should never tolerate any situations in which there is a breach of personal relationships amongst God's people. There is a song composed by a gospel singer, Aunty Clo and it goes thus:

God's own people, (2)

You are a chosen race, a royal priesthood

A holy nation,

Declare the wonderful deeds of God who called you

Out of darkness into his marvellous light.

As God's chosen people, when we have a problem between us, which is normal in every given society, even among animals because they do fight, it should be settled thus:

1) When a person feels hurt, the offender should put it in words to the sinner. There should be face to face personal dialogue, initiated by the person hurt. (It is a difficult thing isn't it but that is God's recommendation)

2) If the two, at that stage cannot understand and reconcile, then again the injured should get a wise person in the community of believers to facilitate the process of reconciliation. Deut. 19:15

3) If this second step does not still work, then the matter again should be taken by the injured to the community of believers and not to the law court. The law courts especially in Cameroon are very corrupt. They are more interested in making money out of the cases than peace. Valuable resources and time is wasted just to end up condemning one person which is not the interest of a Christian community. They judge in love, with the hope of gaining the sinner back to Christ.

4) If he still will not listen, instead of loosing hope, we have to take it to God in prayer. Our earthly relationships do not end in time but into eternity.

Human beings have a limit to forgiveness but Jesus makes us understand that there should be no limit. We are supposed to forgive as long as we have breath because we all have our human fragilities as children of Adam. As others offend us, we also offend others in one way or the other because no human being is perfect. Perfection will only be in the reign of Jesus after his judgement, during his second coming. We are therefore called to forgive those who wrong us, so that those we also wrong will find a place in their hearts to forgive us. In the Beatitudes, Jesus assures us "Blessed are the merciful for they shall obtain mercy".

Divine and human forgiveness goes hand in hand because our vertical relationship (human to God) cannot be good, if our horizontal relationship (human to human) is not good. 1Jn 4:20 makes us understand that: If any one says "I love God", yet hates the neighbour, that person is a lair. A person cannot hate another with whom they see daily and pretend to love God who is Spirit and cannot be seen. Can we count how many times God has been gracious to us? The grace we show to others is nothing compared to the grace of God upon us daily because we sin in words, thought and deeds, knowingly and unknowingly.

We are warned against turning away in hatred and making enemies. We are also warned against revenge because revenge is God's. As difficult and hurting as it may be, the hurt should make the first step to so as to bring transformation.

4. THE STEWARDSHIP OF RECONCILIATION AND RESTORATION AS A CHRISTIAN MISSION

In Gen. 1:26, God said, "Let us make people in our image, to be like ourselves. They will be masters over all life: the fish in the sea, the birds in the sky and all the life stock, wild-animals and small animals". We are therefore created to manage and maintain creation, for which we shall all give account to God for what was entrusted to us.

Human beings have therefore to follow this perfect example of God who in his mercy and grace reconciled to the human race while they were yet sinners by sending Jesus Christ to carry the burden of human sin and thus reconcile every child of Adam to God. Col. 1:15-20 makes us to understand the supremacy of Christ as the head of the body of Christ, who came to reconcile with all, animate and inanimate things.

What human beings are now expected to do, reconciling with one another is just a consequence of divine action. Collins E. Gunton (ed.) in *The Theology of Reconciliation* says, "The sinless Christ is identified with human sinfulness, so that sinful humans may be identified with God's righteousness" This message as an act of reconciliation has been entrusted into the community of God's people, the church of Christ. True love which is sacrificial (Agape), based on truth and not deception should change broken relationships to restored relationships. The Palmist says, how good and pleasant for God's children to live in harmony. This will be an open Bible for non believers to read because "action speaks louder than words".

The Presbyterian Church in Cameroon, in her Book of Orders, has this to say about reconciliation in the Church:

> As a Church, we have a divine task to jealously guard the sovereignty of our nation. We are called upon to promote nation development and national progress. The Churches ministry of love and reconciliation must enhance the general integration. But we must constantly remember that these ideas can only realised in the context of peace. And from our point of view, peace is not only the absence of tension and strife but the presence of justice. That is why the church cannot allow anything to compromise its pursuit of justice.

The aim of Christian stewardship is to reconcile the various levels of God's people in order to do true and successful evangelisation. No human community is conflict free but a Christian community should resolve the problem by non-violence. Martin Luther King Jr., in *Walk for Freedom*, commenting on non violence, as a strategy for reconciliation of Black American in Montgomery declared:

> Along the way of life, someone must have "sense enough" and morality enough to cut off the chain of hate and evil. The greatest way to do that is through love. I believe firmly that love is the transforming power that can lift a whole community to new horizons of fair play, good will and justice.

Justice has to flow like a stream and righteousness like a river among a community of believers. The ability to initiate reconciliation and forgive a member of the community that the evil one has led astray is very important. This relieves pain and clears the conscience of both parties, as they dialogue and come back to talking terms and fellowship in oneness.

> The centre of mission in the 21st Century with a Christian community, be it white, black, Protestants, Roman Catholics, Orthodox, Pentecostals, all those professing Jesus Christ are supposed to be one, (Jn. 17:20-21) so as to promote, encourage and evangelise Jesus Christ. They are supposed to be born again in a divided world. In Ex. 19:5, the Lord, being faithful and just makes a promise to his faith people that, "If you will obey me, keep my covenant, you will be my own special treasure from among all the nations of the earth, for all the earth belongs to me"

The world is fraught with deep divisions in its social and cultural existence, profound inter-national and inter-racial cleavages. In a world like this, the church should proclaim the message of peace, non-violence and reconciliation. The church is in the world though called to be not of the world. Being in the world, the church should not be an island or make itself a holier than thou community. The church must identify with the world, following the example of Christ. Christ humbled himself to receive the baptism of repentance as preached by his forerunner John the

Baptist. This he did to identify himself with sinners in obedience to the father's will to make righteousness available for human beings.

In The Nairobi Declaration, World Assembly IV, 1984, there was a commitment that:

We commit ourselves, as religious men and women, to undertake the work of reconciliation and peacemaking. We must deal with the issue of religious discord where they arise. We must deal with the economic and political struggles which take religious rhetoric for narrow or chauvinistic purposes.

In Eph. 2:11-18, Christ prepared reconciliation by abolishing the dividing walls of hostility between Jews and Gentiles and establishing peace. Christ in Christians should stand against all destructive mountains built up by the human nature in people, groups of people, Christians and non Christians. In Eph. 6: 10-12, we are warned, "For we are not contending against flesh and blood, but against the principalities, against the powers, against the world rulers of this present darkness, against the spiritual hosts of wickedness in the heavenly places". Christians should therefore be united as children of one God to fight and "stand against the wiles of the devil". Christians should be agents of restoration in the world instead of being divided because of our different traditions. Those who win in a Christian race are not the fastest but all who reach the mark. Christians should not be self sufficient with individual salvation but be contented with total societal transformation. They have to offer hope to a broken world of injustice, corruption, tribalism, exploitation, cheating, the rich getting richer and the poor poorer. We must take action, as a multiple-religious body committed to peace, in the very areas where religion and peace seem to be in opposition. Inspired by the exhortation in Eph. 6: 18, the Christian communities everywhere, should be able to identify the various gifts amongst them and pray for discernment of the spirit because reconciliation is by God's power and victory.

From Matt. 22: 37-40, we have the summary of the Ten Commandments given to Moses by God. There we are expected to love God and neighbour, be they enemies, those with whom we do not share the same point of view, male or female, who ever is a neighbour.

5. RECONCILIATION AND RESTORATION IN THE AFRICAN PERSPECTIVE

It is common knowledge that African cultures as opposed to other cultures are most often more human-centred and socially oriented because life is not lived in isolation and there is no individual in the African context. People live as one another's keeper, by sharing in each other's joy or sorrow. People are constantly reminded of of certain expressions like "a person's personality is the behaviour" "A person is evaluated in terms of other people". This reminds the people that a fulfilling life cannot be lived in isolation from fellow human beings. Life with the Africans is possible only in communal relationship in which individuals try to strike a balance between private and social life, thus maintaining a network of relationships with others.

Unlike in our Churches today that reconciliation is gradually dieing down, in a typical African society, (some are influenced by modernisation to think that reconciliation is outdated and people have to mind their individual businesses) reconciliation is very much a alive. They have the wise people of the society headed by the chief or quarter head who meet in a council as need be to listen to conflicts in the community and pass judgement. When found guilty, the person pays a fine for disrupting societal peace according to the gravity of the offence. This is to plead guilty and responsibile for the offence. This is also heavy to the person and memories of the fine will prevent further repetition of the offence subsequently.

There is a whole ritual carried out by the council to reconcile the people. In the West Province of Cameroon for example, the person found guilty is give a stick of broom to clean the tongue and throw behind as prove that the offence will never be repeated and it is gone. They will now look forward for a new and restored relationship. There is breaking of kola nuts by the offended and given to the offender to prove that they are reconciled and can again share the fellowship of eating together again. The two parties embrace each other and the reconciliation process ends with a fellowship meal in the whole community. This is because there is no individualism and once reconciled with the opponent, the society welcomes you in the community. It could get to a climax where the offender refuses to accept the guilt and in this case, you are not integrated into the society. When the crime is beyond human pardon, the person concerned could even be excommunicated from the community.

This we think it is good and Biblical. Reconciliation should not be gotten easily after cost God, the sacrifice of his only begotten son, to suffer pain and humiliation to reconcile the human race with God. Reconciliation is fast dieing in our church communities because it is taken very lightly. When a person comes with a problem, it is not looked into deeply but the people are only consoled, "please forget and forgive for we are all Christians". They forget that we are first human beings before being Christian and when one is offended, there is a deep wound in the heart that needs to be healed. Most often, we cover the wound and pretend that it is healed while the thing eats inside and gets "rotten". At this stage, there is no way to mend and we live in pretence.

By focusing on the centrality of human relationships, it has a contribution to make to the Christian Theology by reminding Christians that any good relationship with God should make an intrinsic link between believing and right doing. This is one of the positive aspects we think that the missionaries to Africa would have exploited to witness to the people. Despite the fact that there are practices and beliefs in the African culture and religion which we should identify as oppressive, there are also a lot that we can use to highlight certain passages in the scriptures and thereby enrich the African Christian Theology.

Reconciliation in the African context is not only between the living but also with the dead. They reconcile with the physical and the spiritual worlds. Mbiti in his book, *African Religion and Philosophy*, makes us understand more of this problem of reconciliation between the living, spirit world and the living dead as an ontological balance, "an ontological balance must be maintained between God and men, the spirits and men, the departed and the living. When this balance is upset, people experience misfortune and suffering or fear that these will strike them." When the living sees that things are not moving the way they wound have wished them to be, they believe that they must be in conflict with the spirit world. As a result, they go offering sacrifices to appease the gods and their ancestors, who they believe mediate between them and the Supreme God, whom they cannot get to directly. After the ritual, balance is restored between the living and the dead and between the spiritual and physical worlds. Due to the African belief in the spirit world, instead of the people taking their problems to the wise in the society, they prefer to take them to those they believe can read the minds and see into the spirit world. Often the problem is solved by some ritual action of purification, cleansing and compensation to both the spirit and the physical worlds.

6. CONCLUSION

Christians are supposed to be truthful in their dealings with one another, supposed to live in peace with strangers, enemies, people of all classes in all aspects of life: Be it economically, socially, politically and religiously. This will bring the community, despite differences and diversities into a common worship, friendship and mission, under the lordship of Christ. Even when we see the other party as a wrongdoer, we cannot forget that we too had done wrong in the past, and the admission and overcoming of that wrong may not have been an easy and direct path for us as well.

God stands at the centre of reconciliation, beckoning us with arms open and saying, "come back to me and I will come back to you", towards a transformation that will allow humanity, one day, to reflect back that divine glory. God brings about reconciliation and we only participate as agents of reconciliation. (II Cor. 5:-20)

When a reconciliation process, successfully goes through, there is peace, which is completeness, fulfilment, maturity, soundness, wholeness, harmony, tranquillity, security, wellbeing, welfare, friendship, agreement, success and prosperity.

BIBLIOGRAPHY

Don, Fleming, *Bridge Bible Directory, An A to Z of biblical information for people of today's World*. Bridge Publications: Australia, 1990.

Alan, Richardson and Bowen, John, (eds.), *A New Dictionary of Christian Theology*. SCM PRESS. LTD. 1985.

Akinson, D. and Field, H. (eds.), *New Dictionary of Christian Ethics and Pastoral Theology*. Inter Varsity Press: England, 1995.

Hunter, J. Rodney, Dictionary of Pastoral Care and Counselling. Abingdon Press, Nashville, 1990.

McFadyen, A. and Sarot, M., (eds.), *Forgiveness and Truth: Explanations in Contemporary Theology*. T & T Clark, Edinburgh and New York, 2001.

Chapman, Geoffrey, *Theology in Reconciliation*. Thomas F. Torrance, Geoffrey Chapman: New York, 1975.

Bromily, W. Geoffrey and co., *The International Standard Bible Encyclopaedia*, Vol. 4William B. Eerdmas Publishing Company, Grand Rapids, Michigan, 1993.

Gunton, E. Collins, (ed.), *The Theology of Reconciliation*. T & T Clark, London. New York, 2003.

Paper of Robert Schrieter, C.PP.S, University of San Diego, Alcala Park, San Diego, 2006.

The PCC, *Book of Orders, Procedure and Practice of the Church*, Press Book: Limbe, 1995.

Mbiti, John, *African Religion and Philosophy*, (2nd ed.), Heinemann: Britain, 1989.

Women in the Ministry of the Church and the Contemporary Challenges

Suzan Mark Zira

1. THE BACKGROUND TO WOMEN IN THE MINISTRY OF THE CHURCH

The Church is the body of believers made up of both men and women, young and old. There are people that follow after the foot steps of Jesus. There are people that have the bible as their guide in every thing. But what of the ministry (service) and women do both men and women receive equal and fair treatment in the ministry of the church? Is it out of way to have women in the ministry of the church? What will be our guide to the question about the position of women in the ministry of the church? How should a woman in the ministry of the church be?

Yes most, if not all of the above questions are going to be addressed in this paper. The ministry of the church is the ministry of God's word and work. And so, we will begin by looking through the bible (word of God) as the background to the study. All through Old and New Testament we have women involve in the ministry of God's word.

We first want to know God's will for mankind right from creation the story of creation tells us that God created both men and women in his image, that is to say both are equal in nature, both were blessed and given dominion. Gen.1:26-30.Says then

God said "let us make man in our image, in our likeness, and let them rule the fish of the sea and the birds of the air, over the livestock, over all the earth, and over all the creatures that move along the ground. So God created man in his own image, in the image of God he crated him male and female he created them. God blessed them and said to them be fruitful and increase in number, fill the earth and subdue it. Rule over the fish of the sea and the births of the air and over every creature that lives on the ground"

> Secondly, the redemption story also made both men and women equal by the special grace of God. Each is forgiven and received eternal life. Each becomes priest with full access to God (1 Peter 2:9.) in him no gender exist, the way of salvation is in the same God (3:28), this is the story of second or new creation through Jesus Christ

Yet, I want us to consider some examples of women of God's word and work in the Old Testament. The first we are to consider is Miriam the sister of Moses called a prophetess and a leader .God himself told Israel that he set before the them leaders Moses, Aaron, Miriam (Micah 6:4 , Exo. 38:8 1Sam 2:22) and other places from the Old Testament prove that there were women who serve at the tabernacle. Deborah the wife of Lapidoth was said to be a Judge, leader and a prophetess (Judges 4:4-5) whom God use to serve the Israelite from their enemies.

Abigail rescued her family by demonstrating great courage and initiative. She gave King David good counsel calling him back to himself and to God. She saves him from taking revenge himself (1sam 25) Hulda was an example, in the time of Josiah, there were prophets like Jeremiah and Zephaniah, yet the king decided to inquire God's will for Israel from Huldah the Prophetess .it was sometimes being thought that women can do certain Jobs only if there are no men available. But that was not the case with King Josiah. He believes that as God speak his mind to men so do he to women. In short there are women in the Old Testament who use their gifts and talent to serve God and to influence their family and nation. Such are also Esther who saved a nation. Moses mother who faithfully taught her son Moses (Musa) the fair of God, Hannah, Ruth and others. They were never forbidden to speak in the public. Women in the Old Testament could make sacrifices on behave of their families (Lev. 1:2). They were allowed to attend feast of the tabernacle (Deut 16: 14; Jud 21:19-21; 11 Kings 5:23).

Jesus attitude to women is worth considering. Jesus God the son taught women as will as men (Luke 10:38-41) There was also a story of the Samaritan woman who had a conversation with Jesus. (John 4:1-42). After this scene, this woman became and Evangelist , it was interesting to note here that Jesus Share that Jesus shared the truth of who he was and forgive her also, she right after the conversation she became an Evangelist through whom many Samaritans were brought to Christ.

Jesus also considers women to be among his close friends (John 11) he let women travel with him during his public ministry. (Mat 27:55 and Luke 8:1-3) shows that, women were among his disciples. He consider them to be among his valid witness (Luke 24:9-11) because women were first to testify to his resurrection. For the resurrected Jesus chose to appear to women, he did not just only appear to them but spoke to them sending them with a message to men (John 20:15-18) this shows that every believer regardless of sex and race has equal access to God for Jesus has broken down the middle wall of partition between us (Eph. 2:14) All division between men and women has been smashed in Jesus.

Therefore, if Jesus himself gave the important Job of proclaiming his resurrection to women and God himself before chose and decided to use a woman to bring forth the saviour, then women in the ministry of the church are doing the right work. The presence of women in the ministry of the church is a sign of obedience to God. If I am not mistaken women were in the ministry of the gospel before the men. Jesus sends them to men with the message when they all lost hope and went back to their various jobs. When then women were still in the ministry of looking for Jesus they had persistence faith. So, it is unfortunate and not true to say that women in the ministry are stepping out of the God's given place.

Moreover, the matching order which is the great commission given by our Lord Jesus Christ to the church is meant to be fulfill by all believers. Go and make disciples of all nation is been given to both men and women. This came to fulfillment at Pentecost when the spirit of God descended on both men and women empowering them for the ministry of the church. The Pentecost is the birth day of the church, both men and women were present when the Holy Spirit came upon them (Act 2:1-4). At the Pentecost, what happened to this group of men and women was that they were filled with the Holy Spirit and began to speck with other tongue. And the ministry of the church had it s beginning from this time with both men and women.

So, I want to say that, women in ministry of the church are not only doing Job that God commands them but also the one he has equip them for. He has given them the resources they need to accomplish in his work. For they have his indwelling spirit who has gifted and enabled them.

2. HINTS ON SOME PROBLEM PASSAGES ABOUT WOMEN IN THE MINISTRY OF THE CHURCH

There are some problem passages in the bible about women in the ministry. These passages stand as an excuse for some denomination when it comes to women involvement in the ministry. Most this writings are found in the writings of Apostle Paul, the great writer of the New Testament books, some of this passages are found in the New Testament were Paul some times say "women should be silence during the church meetings, it is not proper for them to speak. They should be submissive just as the Law says, if they have questions to ask let them ask their husbands at home for it is not proper for a woman to speak in the church meetings" "women should listen and learn quietly and submissive" (1 Cor. 14:34-35; 1 Timothy 2:11) I want us to look at this problem passages from the history of the church in Corinth. Corinth is a great commercial city and the practice of this city was unchristian. They city is a center of business where business men from various places settle for business there. As a result there was gross of immorality, idolatry and division, there was a practice of temple prostitution. With these attitudes and moral confusion Paul establishes a church there. He was always in touch with the Corinthians Christian (act 18:1-7; 1 Cor. 5:9; 11 Cor.12:14) Thus, Paul having established the church and being in touch with them received a disturbing report about this church morality and spirituality. He learns that the believers were struggling with the issues of Division, spiritual immaturity, the role of men and women, immorality and use of spiritual gifts. This moral confusion was affecting this young church. So Paul was writing to solve these problems. As a result he went back to their traditions and culture.

Traditionally, Jewish women were not allowed to take part in religious ceremonies, they were forbidden to speak in the synagogue, they were not allowed in the court of worship in the Jewish temple. These practices were still in existing during the time Paul establish the church in Corinth. Women in many cultures of that time were told to be quite in the Public. They cannot participate in the Heathen rites or attend sacrificial ceremonies. They had always been kept in outer court.

However, the case is reverse in the Christian era. They women were given the privilege to participate in most Christian activities. So women were overjoyed of their involvement, but misused the opportunity. They participate without learning the proper order for the church involvement. They might have been arguing church doctrine without understanding it. They might have been challenging the authority of men without proper knowledge of God's word and will.

Thus there was chaos in the church in Corinth so it is good to note that once an opportunity comes, be careful not to misuse it, for opportunity comes but once. Lack of

Learning proper order is one problem that leads to disorder. Lack of knowledge is a great problem in the life of human beings, that's why God said to Jeremiah, my people perish for lack of knowledge. Be sure of doctrine you teach, in order not to mislead people. More to that it is not right to question the authority of men for it is a God given position. Miriam questioned the authority of her brother Moses and God was angry with her. Be careful not to Question the authority of the man of God. For man as the head reflects the image and glory of God according to (1Corinth 11:8-10.) Instead of questioning the authority of men, we should rather support and uphold it as we work together in God's vine yard.

Paul's solution to this problem was that women should be silent for orderliness in the church meeting. He wrote to encourage the believers as to what is appropriate behavior for Christians. He said this against the confusion and disorderliness. He wrote to encourage the believers as to what is appropriate behavior for Christian. H e said this against the confusion and disorderliness. That let all things be done decently and in order

[1 Corinth 14:40}. This was not said against women in the ministry but against the misused liberty the women have in Christ. The women with the liberty wanted to teach the idea they felt had been revealed to them without appropriate time of learning and testing as was said to timothy in (1Timothy 10-11) that before anyone is appointed deacon he must be given responsibilities to learn the work and must also be tested. This shows that there suppose to be learning of responsibilities and testing of responsibilities and approval before standing to teach. This lack of order was mostly found among women in church of Corinth. This could also be found in the present day churches. So learning and testing is very important to him who waits to work in God's ministry.

Women should always think of what and where they were they were before Christianity to glorify God. I n most cultures before the advent of Christianity women were forbidden to speak in the public. They were not allowed to go religious places, they were seen as less privileged human beings but with the coming of Christianity there is liberty.

Christianity is a religion of liberty, yet it is not a religion of disorder. Therefore misusing of opportunity is destroying you can not know when you claim to know but when ever you humble your self you will learn, the knowledge will surely come, so when you are given freedom let not the freedom destroy God's plan for you. Rather use the freedom, reflecting on what you were and the Grace you are experiencing for Christ sake. Considering God and his will first in your life and position assumed. Not to abused the liberty as the Corinthian women.

However, Paul was not trying to put women out of participating in church activities and the ministry of the gospel not at all, but he talk about having the knowledge first , for one cannot teach in the church without knowing the doctrine of the church, he also talked about using the knowledge appropriately. Knowing is very important as well as you apply it rightly. So Paul was not writing to put women out of participation but he was dealing with the issue of orderliness and appropriation. We can see this from (1 Cor. 11:5) this is the same letter but here he was teaching women how to behave in the church .He says "But woman dishonors her husband if she prays or prophesies with out a covering on her head" which shows that will participate in prayers, prophesy and such like in the church, but they should have a heart felt submission to those who are in authority and husband who is liken to Christ the head of the church. Yes, every woman should see submission as her divine role to her husband and thus, no matter passion of authority assumed, she knows it is temporal. She must be careful not to do things that will dishonor the head who is the husband and her God

Perhaps, some women may misunderstand Paul when he says there is no man or woman; we are all equal before God (Gal.3:28) here Paul did not rule out the divine position of women, but he is talking about the issue grace and salvation. He meant both men and women have sinned and God is also gracious in saving them. So they both can come before God as priest; for Jesus has ushered priesthood of all believers. But not with standing, Christ need order in the church to avoid loud and unruly behavior which may not speak well of their Christianity before the world.

1. Tim 2:8-15 is also a problem passage, this is Paul's instruction to young Timothy a minister at Ephesus where women were not educated, prostitution is also related to religion that fornication haked people with God which shows immorality was encouraged, so Paul instruct Timothy to teach women how to dress, for how one dresses tells of what he/she is. The issue of dressing is very important because as Christian women one should not dress like a prostitute who dresses to attract men; rather Paul encourages women to dress modestly and to the glory of God.

Yes, I as Paul want to say that a Christian woman should know that her dressing represent her before God. For that reason we should not sew any blouse that will expose our body or buy this window laces without preparing a proper under wear under it. Dress for your husband and to the glory of God. Your true attractiveness is your character not worldly display.

More to that, Paul was not stopping women for public participation when he says "let you women keep silence in the churches for it is permitted for a woman to speak, but they commanded to be under obedience as also said the law. And if they will learn anything , let them ask their husband at home" (1.Cor. 14:34-35)

From this passage we can understand that Paul is specifically referring to the people he was writing to. For he said, "let your women keep silence" he did not say all women but the uneducated women of Ephesus, if not, he could have said let women keep silence. Therefore, it is not an excuse to say it is biblical to keep women out of participation in church leadership.

There was also a case of disobedience in Ephesus If not Paul could not have commended them to be under obedience; it is unchristian for a woman to be disobedient. When Paul says women should learn, they should learn about the things of the Lord with all submissiveness to their teachers which he says are their husbands. The best way to learn is to be quite and submissive to the will of the Holy Spirit who is the great teacher. Paul is telling Timothy that it is important to allow the women to learn. Remember in this culture, it was not normally acceptable for women to learn and be taught any thing, so the issue was to encourage the women to learn as men. What they were to learn was the nature of God and how to live a godly life, by so doing they can teach what they know not teaching out of ignorance.

Furthermore, Paul was not against women teaching doctrine, but he was against them teaching doctrinal standards which was already established by the apostolic teaching (Acts 25) we can see the prove of this in his writing to (Titus 2:3-4) where he told older women to teach the younger ones. Therefore, to learn in silence is referring to the women maintain themselves with dignity and order in the service. For it is important for any one who will teach, to have good and solid understanding of the scriptures and doctrine. Every Christian woman can tell of excitement in Christ and what has happen to he, but not to teach. For one to teach he must first of all learn, that is why Paul said to Timothy (2 Timothy 2:15) "study to show your self approve unto God, a workman that needed not to be shamed, rightly giving the word of the truth" this means it take much learning before one can rightly know the truth and teach others. If we are to relate this to the women of Ephesus, Paul was writing to, there were some definite problems that were not allowing these unlearned women to teach. But it is not applicable to every woman.

One more reasons why Paul tells women to learn in silence is the issue of false doctrine. There were false teachers that went about deceiving people that women were also mediators between God and men so Paul in (1 Timothy 2:5) addressed this doctrinal error that only Christ is the mediator, while all believers can pray to God directly. Paul had the fear, that women may assume this position falsely that they are a mediator, which was why he said women should be properly instructed in the biblical ways before they could teach others. Paul was not trying to lower them below men; rather, he was trying to help them have scriptural principle while seeking to maintain a godly and holy order in the church.

Therefore, I call upon every Christian woman to have the approval of our master Jesus. As Mary whom he said, had chosen the best (Luke 10:42) Mary had that approval because she sat submissively to learn about God and godly life. Lets first give ourselves to learning after which we can teach what we have learnt. Never be abstracted by position and power seeking. It will come at God's appointed time. Jesus said, Martha was abstracted by temporal things

3.   THE CONTEMPORARY CHALLENGES

I want to begin by saying that as believers in the lord Jesus Christ, our pursuit of the ministry or any other goal in our lives should never be based on selfish ambition or wrong desire (Philippians 1:6, 2:5) instead it should only be our obedience to God's call considering only his priority for our lives, our families and his church. With this in mind, what ever challenges we encounter in the ministry as we will see some below we should not be discouraged

Therefore, some of the contemporary challenges we meet as women in the ministry of the EYN church are as follows.

- Women in the ministry are seen by some people as stepping into men's work, that the ministry of the church is for the men, because of that women are seen as threat. This is because most people see working in the ministry as a way to assume Lordship or kingship position, not knowing that it is a position of service. It is good to note that any one working in the ministry of the church has assumed position of service to the people

- Transfer- men in the ministry of the church can be transferred easily and to do any work. But that is not the case with women, because their place of work is limited. They are only allowed to teach or work with TEE or Literacy programmes in EYN. They can't be posted to work in church or DCC (district church council) Secretary This is seen as work that can only be done by men, the reason is not well stated

- Ordination – this is seen EYN as a responsibility only for men not women. The funniest part of this is that women teach the men in the Bible schools and the theological college on how to become pastors, but they themselves can not be pastors, some even see it as a divine privilege given only to men. I want to observe that if on is ordained to be a pastor over people, I is good to note that the name pastor in Greek means shepherds. And the word shepherds in the real sense means feeding the sheep, caring for the sheep, nurturing the sheep or binding their wounds. All these refer to what is to be done to church members. It does not mean an office but the work, and the work sounds mothering instead of fathering.

- Seminars, retreat and conferences are organized for Pastors and Evangelist but none has ever been organized in respect of women in the ministry. In short I want to say that the position of women in the ministry is not well specified in EYN. The Pastors are located seats, their wives and evangelist as well, but I have never heard of a location of seat in a gathering for a woman in the ministry. The presence of your students just because you are not recognized can cost you your seat. The Usher will ask you to leave your seat for your former student and they will comfortably occupy it. In most cases church occasions Pastors and their wives and the evangelist are welcomed and introduced but not a woman in the ministry

- However, I am not blaming men for treating women in such a way, some are still under the influence of culture which is men dominated. I only want to call the attention of the church to look into this things mention above as well as the formation of each committee at the national level through DCC to LCC levels and see what I am talking about whether I am talking sense. Women also have a share in the blame for they are the majority in the church, but when it comes to nomination and election, they don't vote their fellow women. So, I call that lets prove our capability among women wherever we fine ourselves.

THE WAY FORWARD AND CONCLUSION

The above challenges have brought fear and discouragement to women in the ministry and even those wishing to join the ministry. But I wish to say that you should remember your call. God who calls you into the ministry will see you through all difficulties such are tests to strengthen you faith. Depend on his spirit to lead your way.

Our cultural believe that women are to be seen and not to be heard, for that they expect women even in the ministry to be passive, submitting without questioning the authority of men. Yes, we should submit to God given authority but not to be passive. If possible wherever you fine yourself make your presence to be known positively and orderly, don't be mute as though you are not a life.

Many people are saying that women can not make good and correct decisions, as such equalized to children. Women work to prove them wrong. For decision making is part of every human being. Right decisions are always don under leadership of the Holy Spirit. Remember, King Solomon asked God for the Spirit of discernment, to be able to know right form wrong. God gave him and in abundance. The same could be the portion of any true Christian Don't see yourself as doing the wrong Job. For if our Lord Jesus commanded Mary who was ready to be his disciple than Martha. (Luke 40:11) then, we who have chosen to be in the ministry of the church have made best choice. It is a choice of life and to give life. Let's be sure we become women of influence in whatever position we fine ourselves. There is Misconception of leadership for most people see it as ruler ship position. Some of us are opportune to be in leadership position, so prove your position by influencing and serving people.

In conclusion, the ministry of the church is for both men and women, the Bible did not limit the service to a particular nation, tribe, clan, or gender. This is a ministry God set a part both men and women from all nations for it. Fire on!

BIBLIOGRAPHY

George, Elizabeth, Women after God's own Heart, (Eugene, Or.:Harvest House), 2007.

Cayang, Felicia Kanneng, Matan da suka yi tafiya tare da Allah, (Jos: Copro Media), 1999.

Mark Suzan, God Speaks to through Women. (Jos: Ade Printing Press), 2003.

Taege, Marlys, Women through the Bible: devotions for women's groups, (St.Louis: Concordia Publishing House), 1987.

Samuel, Rebeccah, Women in the ministry with Jesus, (ANET production), 2000.

Vickie Kraft, Women Mentoring Women: ways to start, maintain, and expand a biblical women's ministry, (Chicago: Moody Press), 1992.

Wendy and Frank, Women as Minister and Leader, ACTS International Edition Vol. 27. 1999.